THE DAY I LEARNED TO PUMP GAS

FINDING THE LIGHT THROUGH THE DARKNESS

TM MOORE

Instagram: tmmoore17
Blog: bepowerfulmedia.com
Substack: lemonade
TikTok: tmarconmoo

POWERFUL BOOKS

Published by Powerful Books.

ISBN 978-1-83522-032-0 (eBook)

ISBN 978-1-83522-033-7 (PB)

ISBN 978-1-83522-034-4 (HC)

How many times can you get broken down, kicked to the curb, and stand up to reinvent yourself? What does it take to restart, face your fears, and do it all again? How can you find strength in yourself to do this over and over again?

When you look back on your life, do you see the signposts that lit the way each time you had to change direction or choose a different path, can you see the way forward clearly? Looking back is easier than looking forward. What did those moments look like? Were you running from danger or moving towards safety? This book talks about my life, my childhood, and beyond motherhood. The grief, abuse, and loss I went through over and over, and each time, I stood stronger and taller.

I learned to know Jesus from a very young age, even before I knew his name. He was there with me, guiding me and walking with me through my journey. Looking back on my path, I know I was never on it alone.

This is my journey of grief and abuse, with acceptance, forgiveness, clarity, and faith.

I would like to thank my children and husband for, without judgment, helping me be honest and open about my story and giving me strength, courage, and bravery. I also want to thank my priests for their insight, words, encouragement, and enduring Presence. Perry, Emma, and the Powerful Book community for helping me navigate this journey and sending me on a path of healing.

I would like to dedicate this book to my younger sister, who passed away before she had a chance to tell her story; this is why I am telling mine. And to everyone who mourns their lost childhood. A Faithful journey can bring strength, forgiveness, clarity, and a chance to move forward from darkness into the light.

CONTENTS

Standing at the gas station with my husband as he showed me the simple task of putting gas in my car, I knew, in that single moment, the course of my life was changing. I would be a widow, a single parent. Death, grief, loss, and heartache were again coming. This moment had been coming for ten years, ten years of slowly losing my husband.

My story starts before the beginning, as most stories often do.

PART 1
MY STORY

ONE
THE RED TRICYCLE

My childhood was filled with innocence, adventure, and curiosity. We were a close family and spent a lot of time together. It was far from perfect, but looking back now, it was the happiest time of my life.

When I was a toddler, I had a dog named Saber. She was a beautiful golden color. I remember the feelings I felt for her, the feel of her fur, remembering loving her so much I could burst, playing in the back garden with her, rubbing and petting her. I must have been three years old when she got sick. I don't recall all the details, just that my parents took her to the vet, and she didn't come home. I vividly remember standing on my front doorstep and waving goodbye to Saber. She was in a basket, surrounded by angels; they were taking her up to heaven. As a three-year-old, my mind was making sense of something my heart couldn't understand. I was four when we moved, I remember riding my red tricycle down the street to our new home. I was not allowed to cross the road, so I didn't get too far. I watched as our stuff was being loaded into the big van. I figured I could beat the van there if I rode fast enough! My youngest sister and I would share a bedroom. We had this purple wallpaper with swirly patterns and dolls, and our wardrobe was between our beds. We would take turns knocking nursery rhyme tunes on it, trying to guess which one it was, telling stories, and singing songs to each other at night. I often hid toys and books under my pillow at night and would often read by the street lamp shining on my walls. I would lay awake for hours waiting for my dad to come home from work, staring out of my front bedroom window, looking at the empty, dark streets, making up families and stories. I would duck into bed when I saw my dad's car pull up. Only then could I sleep. My best friend lived next door to us. We used to play water games in the sink at his house, chase each other around the backyards, climb fences, walls, and trees, and build forts out of sticks and leaves. In the mornings, I would eat porridge at his house, a large hot bowl mixed with milk and golden syrup, and walk to school together. One scorching Summer, we had a plastic pool in the back garden. My mum also gave us a massive box of fancy dress-up clothes. My sisters and I would put them on and lay in the pool. We pretended we were princesses or mermaids in a secret garden with fancy clothes floating around us. My mum would get mad and throw the clothes that went in the pool away, so we didn't have them for long! We lived in terrace council homes, all snuggled together up a steep hill. The kitchen was at the front, and I often saw my mum cooking and having a smoke while we played on the green outside. The back gardens were all long and separated by broken chain-link fences. There was a garden shed by the house, which my mum had turned into a school/doll house. It housed all our games, toys, and dolls and had a desk where I would pretend to write lessons. The top of the garden was brambles and mud. I would scoot in there, pretend I was on wild adventures, getting scratched up by thorns, trying to tempt myself to taste the berries that grew on them. My mum told me if I ate just one, I would die. This terrified me but also intrigued me. When my elder sister started school, I missed her so much. I would watch my cartoons in the mornings while eating Weetabix with crunchy sugar and would then wait until it was time for her to come home. I couldn't tell the time, but my mum showed me where the hands on the clock would be when she came home. My mum would have her friends come over for coffee in the mornings. They drank tea, but called it coffee mornings from the American shows they watched. The kitchen would be a haze of cigarette smoke and chatter. I would hear the kettle whistle, the tea cups clink, and the chatter of grown-up voices. I would go into the kitchen and make my way to my mum; she had soft, dark curly hair and a warm lap. Listening to the grown-up talk, I felt privileged, like I was a part of something big and vital. After a while, though, I would become antsy and fidgety, bored at the conversations I couldn't keep track of. I needed color and movement, so I would slink back out and play outside.

Our house was midway up a steep hill, with a small parking area at the bottom. We would skateboard down our road and shoot under the parked cars. Laying under the vehicles, we had to shimmy our way out, getting covered in grease and gravel. I remember lying under the cars, looking at the underworking; they smelled so thick and heavy. We would try to jump off our skateboards before they went under and ended up being propelled down the hill and steps before flying on the concrete. The scabs on my knees and elbows were like badges of honour. One summer, when I was about six or seven, our dad made my older sister and I stilts. They were big yellow wooden ones with wooden foot supports. We would have races on them. I was running up the streets, down the hills, and jumping down the stairs. Mine were much shorter and circular, they had a rubber grip at the top to hold on to. My sisters were much bigger and rectangular, they didn't have rubber grips, so when I jumped on them, I always got these huge splinters in my hands. Jumping on my sister's stilts was like trying to get on a bike that was too big. I had to stand on the wall, lean them in front of me and jump on them. My stilts would tower above me, and my hands gripped the middle part. I was so high up that I felt powerful. The neighborhood kids would beg for a turn. We had hours and summers full of fun on them. There was a kind of chalk pit close to us. It was a dug-out niche at the back of the park. It was hidden from the prying eyes of our parents. It was full of tree stumps, roots, rocks, and hunks of large porous chalk. We were not allowed to go there, but we did! Using old cardboard boxes, we would climb the area and shoot down the chalk, trying to avoid the rocks and roots; we would end up battered and filthy. Walking home, trying to clean ourselves up, and pretending nothing had happened. Often, we took chunks of chalk and drew hopscotch on the pavements or silly messages on walls. At school, there was a concrete train. I was the only girl who could climb to the top of this train. It was awesome! I would throw my shoes and socks off and climb the train barefoot. I was always getting scrapes on my knees and elbows. I would shrug my shoulders and pretend innocence when my parents asked how I was always so dirty and scratched up. I came out of school one afternoon when I was about four or five, and I saw my dad's mum standing there, wearing big flashy glasses and huge red curly hair; she smelled like softness and love. I yelled out, "That's my Nan, that is."

I ran straight into her skirt and gave her a huge hug. Years later, she told me that was the moment she knew! We adored each other. She became my person, my pen pal. We would send letters with funny poems of Gnus. I would spend weeks at her house, watching the clock, being warm, watching old movies, and eating rum raisin ice cream.

We were never Christened as kids, but there was a church close to where we lived. I would beg my mum to take me. I was supposed to go downstairs for the children's programs, but that confused and bored me, so I would sneak back up, hide behind the pews at the back, and flip through the pages of the Bibles. They smelled old and dusty, the pages thin and the words and sentences never made any sense. Those pages held so much intrigue for me; I wanted to read the words and unravel the mystery they held.

I never understood school, I would lose track of what the teacher said and what I was supposed to do. I preferred staring out the window, my mind wandering into daydreams and thinking about all my adventures. Except for reading, I loved to read; I would become so wrapped up and lost in the stories. I loved reading my mum's books at home, Catherine Cookson and PD James. I did have a teacher I adored. She had the same birthday as me. I remember giving her a huge pop-up card full of pink roses. I remembered her birthday every year until I forgot.

My dad was a driver; he would often have parcels to deliver hours away. I loved going with him, watching the world go by with the night sky, sleeping to the hum of the car traveling down the motorways.

I was quite athletic, running, climbing trees, obstacle courses, and gymnastics, I was agile and fast. There was a local gymnastics club I belonged to, and I was well aware that my parents struggled to pay the fees. I pretended to lose interest and dropped out but continued at schools and local competitions. When I was ten, we moved again to a much bigger house, it would be our last childhood move. I now had my own room. It was the second biggest room in the house and probably the coldest, with bare floorboards and torn wallpaper. My mum got carpet scraps and made a walking path from my door to the window and bed, I covered my walls with posters of pop stars from magazines. I would keep my jammies and school clothes in my bed to keep the cold and dampness off and had this huge life-size stuffed dog which I would snuggle and stay warm with. The winter mornings were the worst. I could see my breath in my room, and the frost covered the inside of the windows. I would dress in bed and then hopscotch on my bits of carpets out of my room. Head down to the living room where the fire was on, sit, and warm up. My mum would be heating milk. I would pour it over my Weetabix; they become warm and soggy, the sugar melting a bit. I could feel the heat warm me as I ate them.

I made new friends in the neighborhood, and summers saw us by the river or the canal. Catching tadpoles, paddling, wading in the rushes, and getting soaked with mud slime! I like to visit the horse and cow fields, feed them apples and tall grass, and make friends with them. I knew someone who helped out at a stable and was allowed to ride the horses. I went a few times. The stables smelt like thick mud, wet straw, and the musky smell of horses. We were allowed to ride once we had finished mucking the stables out. Climbing onto and sitting on the huge horse was quite a feat. We went from a slow trot to a cantor. I felt terrified and excited at the same time. It seemed like I had lost control of the horse, but he felt calm and controlled, trotting around the fenced-in field. One time I saw my friend, she had a whip in her hand and was yelling at the horse she was on with her arm stretched behind her, she kept whipping and shouting angrily at the horse. It was pretty horrifying to see. Once we were finished and settling the horses back down, I walked over to the one she had whipped. I looked into his big brown eyes, leaned my face onto his nose, and felt his hot breath coming from his nostril. I whispered sweet words of love to him. Hoping he would forget the pain of being whipped.

On Saturday mornings, I would run downstairs, and my mum would be there with a steaming cup of tea and a warm fire, and we would watch the beachcombers together. Often, a letter had come from my nan; I would read it to myself, giggling at her funny words before passing it to my mum to read. She would read it aloud, laughing at all the silly bits. My mum had this full-length zip-up dressing gown; it was warm and fuzzy, and I loved snuggling into her. I felt safe and warm. For me, the epitome of love was in my mother's arms. I adored her and loved her. I would play with her hands in the evening and sneak into her bed when I couldn't sleep. I used to love watching her bake. She was such a great cook and made everything from scratch. Her pastry was amazing, flakey, and buttery, meat pies, sausage rolls, and mince pies, she made the best toad-in-the-hole, the batter was so huge and crispy, with mashed potatoes and gravy. That was my comfort food: mashed potatoes and gravy, a creamy mash made with warm milk and butter, real gravy made from stock, and Sunday dinner drippings. My mum's fried chicken, though, oh my! To this day, I still crave her fried chicken and salad. I crave the taste and feeling of eating it. I have yet to find the perfect blend of tastes. It was like warm, lightly seasoned, crunchy softness that filled my mouth with the cold tart crunch of cucumber and salad cream. These flavours would blend and make a memory I am still trying to catch.

Over time, I had a carpet fitted, and my mum decorated my bedroom with dark blue flowers on one side and a textured pale blue wallpaper on the other. I didn't love the look at first; I never wanted to be a girly girl, and flowers to me were girly, but in the years after, I craved to see the room she made for me.

On my tenth birthday, my mum called me into their bedroom. As I walked in, I saw unwrapped Liverpool gear all over the bed. Scarf, hat, towel, bag, shirts. It was a sea of beauty! I screeched with delight and dove onto the bed, wrapping myself up in all my birthday gifts. I felt so much love and pride on that birthday. They really got me! They really understood and knew me. I donned my new scarf and Liverpool bag to school, hanging it on the hook for everyone to see. The girls were a bit mean; they all had the Barbapapa, Holly Hobby, and pink girly bags. I was a bit embarrassed while at school, but walking home, I was queen of the world! Why couldn't they understand a girl could love and be good at sports, have a favorite footy team, wear jeans and trainers, and be muddy all the time?

TWO

TWO SIDES OF THE SAME COIN

How can death look and feel so different? When an elderly sick person dies after suffering years of pain, immobility, and aphasia, it can be a relief and freedom from suffering. But a healthy baby, just learning to walk and talk, with the entire world at his feet, dies for no apparent reason. It feels like an entire lifetime has been stolen, the ghost of someone they will never become.

When I was about twelve, my baby cousin died; he was two years old. He was incredibly cute, with chubby cheeks, a cheeky smile, and soft, mousy blond hair. I didn't think there was a more adorable baby in the world! He was my dad's brother's son. They lived further north than us and we would visit on the school holidays. I remember my uncle phoning and having him speak on the phone when he was starting to talk. It's all hazy, but I remember having to drive with my mum to pick up my dad from work, which was weird as my dad was a taxi driver! I remember sitting in my mum's car, watching my dad leave the office. He seemed pretty normal at first, so I thought everything was good. Then, the closer to us he got, the more he just seemed to collapse; his head sank low and his knees began to buckle, he broke down in the car into a heap of wailing tears. My mum leaned over and held him. I remember being confused and asking if my baby cousin was okay. My dad couldn't talk; he was sobbing. My mum said she would speak with us later.

I wasn't sure exactly what was happening. It wasn't very clear. My heart felt full and achy, and my head was hot and confused. Was he okay? Was he dead? What happened? My dad left that night and drove straight to their place. My mum didn't really know what to say. This whole time is very fuzzy. I remember being told he was sick in his sleep. I could not get my head around this. When the funeral came, we were not allowed to go; I begged and begged to. I needed to see and understand what was happening. I am unsure who cared for us when my parents drove up. I remember my dad showing me a giant yellow flower teddy, saying that it was from us all. My heart was breaking; I had many questions and felt stunned and numb. I wanted to go to the funeral and I was pretty upset and mad that I couldn't. My parents were reticent about the whole thing. My mum would talk to me a little when I asked questions. But everything seemed so vague and confusing. I don't remember visiting them for quite a long time. It was my first experience with death, apart from my animals. The thoughts and images would invade my sleep, my daily thoughts. It was confusing. I was forever waiting for snippets of information, piecing together my own version of events. My dad's mum, my nan, would talk to me the most about it, but even then, she would clam up and change the subject.

My mum's mum was sick for as long as I knew her; she had her first stroke when she was twenty-nine years old. I never knew her to be able to talk or walk well.

My mum's dad, my grandpop, smelled like love and tobacco. He used to stomp around the house, looking for his cold cups of tea. He would have loose tea leaves and cold tea skin floating on the top of his tea. He smoked roll-ups, and I remember them always being so tiny and stained yellow that he often had one stuck to the corner of his bottom lip. There were always tobacco tins in his kitchen and sitting room, with burnt-out roll-ups. When we visited, my grandpop would rattle his oily and tobacco-stained hands in his pocket. Sometimes, he found 10p, one for each of us. How often did I drop that 10p in my mouth, taste the dirty metallic coin, and choke? We took care of my nana sometimes to give my grandpop a break. She would go to a day center a few days a week and do crafts there. One time, she made a crochet clown and sewed pre-cut teddy bears. One of these bears, a black and white panda, my grandpop would sleep with at night to keep himself warm; I claimed it when he passed. She couldn't talk or walk very well. She had so many strokes by the time I was born and had a pacemaker. She scared me a little, as I didn't understand her much. We used to visit most Sundays. If she were up, I would sit with her. I wanted to ask her questions about her life; I felt shy and intrusive; it was tough to understand what she was saying. She would mouth words, and only sounds would come out. I would try to figure out what she was saying. I always tried to be patient and understanding. But I was usually a bit scared of her. It made me feel weird. I loved her, and I loved being close to her.

One time, at their house, we were having Sunday dinner. My sisters and I were likely bickering and messing around at the table. We were not allowed to have our elbows on the table and had to hold our cutlery a particular way. My nan yelled out "Stop!!"

Like so loud and angry. I was stunned, terrified, and also a little impressed. She spent a lot of time in the hospital; we would pop by and visit. I remember it smelling quite clinical and a bit like pee. I felt timid and self-conscious walking through the corridors. My nana looked so small in the hospital bed. All I remember is seeing her mass of gray curly hair, her big crooked Jewish nose, and her strong outlined mouth. She looked tiny. My parents and grandpop would sit with her and chat. I got bored quite easily and just looked around. I found it hard to look at my nana. She looked so weak. I remember feeling a bit scared, sad, and self-conscious. She looked so helpless and frail. I was afraid to touch her, to kiss her goodbye. I always did though; her skin felt soft and papery. I tried to give all my love and words in those kisses' goodbyes. My heart wanted to say so much. But my childhood mouth couldn't make out the words.

I remember sitting in my room one day, looking out of my window. I saw my mum's sister and her husband pull up outside. My aunt never came to visit.

She rarely left her house; she only lived a few minutes' walk away and we would pop down most days. To see her outside my house was very unusual. I felt a rush of excitement that she had come to visit. I saw a flash of her face; she wore a frown and looked serious and worried. I knew in an instant what had happened. My nana had died. No one needed to tell me. I felt a crushing pain in my gut, like a cold punch; I curled up in a ball and started sobbing. Then, as quickly as it came, it went. I felt a peacefulness, a warmth. My nana was no longer suffering; she was at peace. I felt that peace. I felt that overall thankfulness that she could be at rest now. It felt like a loving glow around me; even though I knew so little about religion and God, it felt like Jesus had come and taken my Jewish nana home. She was safe and free. My mum came into my room; I said I know! I was crying, but I felt the peacefulness. I don't remember going to her funeral either. Or what exactly happened afterward? I remember being okay with her death. She had suffered for most of her adult life. She deserved some peace.

THREE
MY MUM

My mum and I had a bond that was unbreakable. When she passed, it was as though the essence of life had been ripped away, leaving behind a profound and inconsolable ache in the very depths of my heart.

I loved my mum. As children, we love our parents. They are our whole worlds. My mum though, we were like one, I often didn't know where she ended, and I began. My favorite place was to be near her, snuggled next to her in bed, watching TV while I traced the lines of her hands with my fingers. I loved her scent, a subtle mix of cigarettes, tea, and Chantilly perfume. The way her mouth moved when she laughed. She had hazel eyes, cream-colored skin, and thick black curly hair. I loved that I also had hazel eyes, but my skin has always been pale. She listened to Kim Carnes and Rod Stewart on the record player and danced as she cleaned the house. My mum practiced Yoga a few times a week; I would join her sometimes. I was very flexible and agile, but I was seriously impressed with what my mum and her friends could do. As a pre-teen girl, parents seemed so old, and watching them ease into a lotus position without barely trying was seriously impressive. My mum was strong and didn't put up with nonsense and would call it; if it were bullshit, she would say it was bullshit. She was strong and outspoken. We could talk about anything. She worked in a betting shop on Saturdays. Kids were not allowed in, but sometimes, I would sneak around the back and peek into the door. It was dark and very smokey in there; they had small TVs all around the room, and I would see men glued to the screens, yelling, cheering, and jeering at them. My mum would spot me, sneak me into the break room for a few minutes, make me a cup of tea, and then shoo me off before we both got into trouble. In the evenings, after dinner, my sisters and I had jobs to clean up before we could sit and watch TV. We would wash, dry, and stack the dishes while listening to the small radio; it often took longer if our favorite songs came on. Once finished, we would pile into the sitting room. The fire was blazing; cigarette smoke filled the air. We had a gorgeous German shepherd called Dax at this time, and he would be snuggled on the floor. The three of us would find our cozy place and settle in for an hour or so of TV. Once in a while, my mum or dad would ask us to light their cigarettes on our electric stove top. It felt like our eyes and nose would be singed as we moved close to light the cigarette. In the mornings, I would bring my mum a cup of tea in, even on school days. She loved strong, sweet tea, she would sit in bed, drink tea, and smoke her cigarette; we would talk about my day ahead and what book she was reading. I loved to read her books once she had finished them. She would often be hosting or going to her coffee mornings. Most days, she would make her way to her sister's house. She lived a few minutes' walk away, and I would find them there after school most days, chatting and laughing away. My mum and her sister were so close that a day didn't go by without them chatting for at least a few hours.

As I entered my teen years, I needed my identity and started pulling away. I wanted to define myself and figure out who I was apart from my mum. I became surly, and as a thirteen-year-old girl, hormones were rushing through my body. I could go from laughing to screaming to floods of tears in moments. I started to become embarrassed of my mum, not ashamed in a shame-like way, but embarrassed in a "wanting to be a grown-up, and not needing you." My mum was an amazing cook. Her food was so warm and comforting. She would cook for us every night; the smell of food, sausages, lamb chops, and meat pies constantly came from our kitchen. Sunday mornings saw my older sister and I running down to the paper shop to pick up the Sundays and our weekly comics. Usually, we were allowed to get a pack of polos. The dilemma of picking fruit or mint was the most challenging part!

My mum loved Rod Stewart, and we would play and dance to his records all the time; we also loved watching the evening TV shows. I went on a school camping trip once; it was a nightmare, cold, muddy trip, and it made me miserable. My highlight was getting a letter from my mum. She gave me an update on our favorite show. She told me she loved and missed me. I wish I had kept that letter. I did for years, but over time, it became lost. My mum and dad would have a lunch date every Wednesday. I was able to go a few times when I was off sick from school. I remember sitting in the cafe above the paper shop, making towers out of sugar cubes. Any day I could be next to Mum was my best day. My parents fought a lot; there was so much tension and sadness in my house. Money issues were big; my dad was quite needy and selfish, and my mum was fiercely independent. I would stay in my room, listening to records, hanging out with my older sister, watching her put her make-up on, doing her hair, and listening to all her stories and adventures of being a teenager. I would play teddies and board games with my younger sister or lie on her bed, looking at books and comics.

One night, when I was thirteen and having a particularly bitchy day, Mum made dinner. Chicken legs, boiled buttered potatoes and salad I think. She was not feeling well and struggled to make it. The table was set and we were all eating, but my mum was lying on the couch. She did not look well at all. I was angry and annoyed at her for not joining us at the table. We were all eating, and she was lying on the couch. I went to her, she looked pale and awful. I was a bit scared, but my pre-teen sass took over. These words that will echo in my mind forever. These were the last words I ever spoke to my mum. “If you die, it’s your own fault for smoking.”

I stormed upstairs, horrified at what I had just said. My ears burned and my head felt dizzy and nauseous. I was such a shit for saying such awful words. I wanted to go down and say something different. But I was frozen to the spot. I couldn’t move.

I heard yelling and screaming; my dad and older sister were yelling. A bath was running. I was told to run down and get my aunt right away. Urgent. There was so much screaming in the house, the bath was running, screaming, crying, noise. I flew out of the house and started running to my aunts. My head was spinning. Time was coming and going, and I couldn’t understand anything. I felt like I was running but getting nowhere. Suddenly, my aunt and cousin pulled up. My aunt yelled at me... “What are you doing? Why are you out here?”

I was confused. Was I in trouble? I was coming to get you? What is happening? I can't remember if I ran back home or got in the car. I do remember going to a friend's house up the street and sitting in someone's bedroom. I was hunched in the corner, watching the TV. It was dark except for the noise of the TV. I was a bit confused. Why was I here? Where were my mum and dad? My older and younger sisters were downstairs, I believe. I remember sitting there, confused, trying to determine what was happening. Then the pain started. It felt like my body was being ripped apart. Like my soul was extracting itself. The pain was searing, cramping, and torturous. I felt like I was vomiting my entire self. I knew, I knew at that moment, that my mum was gone. She was gone. I would never be able to reach her again. Never be able to tell her I loved her, smell her, hold her, hug her. She was gone. I was over. I sat in the dark. It seemed like hours and minutes, all at the same time. I was terrified. I was terrified that someone would come and tell me what I knew was true. I had felt her die. I had felt her life leave my body in a searing, painful way. There was a knock at the door, and I was called downstairs. It was my dad. He had come to pick up me and my younger sister. He didn't say much; he just took our hands and walked us down the street to our house. On the way down, I asked how Mum was. Where is she? He told me everything was going to be okay; She was at the hospital. Was I wrong? I breathed a sigh. Everything was going to be okay. It's okay. It was all a mistake. Mum is at the hospital. I was wrong. Everything is fine. I felt relief. I could breathe. My dad grabbed my hand tightly as we went inside the house.

Everyone was there: my aunts, mum's friends, and dad's cousins. What the hell was going on? People were cleaning the kitchen and sitting down. No one was talking. What is going on? As I looked at everyone's face, I knew. It was not a mistake. My mum had died. My moment of relief was gone. My ears started to thunder; I couldn't breathe. Those last words were screaming in my head. People were trying to get me to sit down. I didn't want to bloody sit down. My younger sister was crying. I heard my dad screaming and banging something. I ran through the house to the back garden. Cool air. I could breathe. My head was screaming, but no words came. Tears were welling up inside; my heart ached, and it felt like it was going to burst. I ran around the garden, or did it feel like I just did. I wanted everyone to leave. Why were people all here? Leave! I think my older sister came out and got me. I went inside with her, and someone pulled me on their lap. They put their arms around me, and I just sank in and started to sob. Someone said something like "It's good she is crying; she will be fine now."

I heard those words, and anger yelled up inside. I pulled my sobs in. My hair was sticking to my face; snot was mixed with tears on my face. My head inside my head, I shook and said, "No! No! This was not going to happen."

I pulled away, took a breath, and said, "No."

I don't remember what I said next, but it was cruel and hurtful, and I ran upstairs to my room. My sisters and I went to my dad's cousin's house after. All the girls were sleeping in bed. I remember sliding into my 2nd cousin's bed. Quietly so as not to disturb her. She awoke, she said quietly. "Is it true?"

My mind raced, and my body went numb. "Is what true?" Thinking I would actually have to say those words!!

"Are you a woman now??" she asked.

I was confused about what she meant; I couldn't think of what she was talking about, so I just said,"Yes."

The next few days were so blurry. I wanted to be with my aunt. No one was saying anything. It was strange and motionless. I had to ask a friend to take over my paper round for that week. I told her I had a funeral to go to. She laughed a bit and said I always had funerals to go to... she had helped me with my cousins and my nana's funerals the months and year before. I looked at her, not wanting to speak, feeling dizzy and nauseous. I blurted it out. "It's my mum."

She looked at me and ran inside her house. I felt like my world was crashing around me. I ran down the hill to my aunt's house. There were people in her kitchen. I just looked at them; I couldn't breathe and had to escape. And I ran through her house to the back garden. The days before the funeral were strange. I remember my dad showing me a poem to put on her headstone and picking out a headstone. I was given some money to buy something to wear. It was all strange and normal. We all wrote letters to Mum, sealed, and put in her coffin. I barely remember what I wrote. It was a mix of song lyrics, tears, and words. The night before the funeral, I stayed with my aunt. We sat up most of the night reading Agatha Christie's books and figuring out who had done it. We did not talk about the next day. I fell asleep in the early hours. I was woken up and told to get dressed. My mum was at home. They laid the coffin in the family home the night before the funerals. I didn't want to be there. I didn't want to go. My older cousin told me that if I changed my mind, to let her know, and she would take me, no questions asked. I decided to go at the last minute. I kept thinking in my head, what would I regret more, seeing or not seeing her? I have always been indecisive, but I didn't want to get this wrong. We decided to go. She went in first. I slowly crept into the room. My mum looked like she was asleep. I was dressed in her favorite dress. She didn't look like the mum I had in my heart. I couldn't see the thing that made her my mum; maybe I was still trying to tell myself that this was not real. I blurted out, "That's not my mum," and ran out of the room.

The funeral was a blur. There are so many people, so many cars, so many doors of houses\shops open with people standing watching the parade of cars go by. I didn't want anyone to see me. We had to drive by my high school on the way to the cemetery; I hid my head in case anyone I knew was looking. It was early September, and school had just started after the summer. At the cemetery, there were so many people around. I couldn't hear anything; my heart was pounding in my ears. I was instructed to kneel, pick up some dirt, and throw it on her coffin. What! I couldn't do that! I yelled out; "I am not throwing mud on my mum!"

I got up and left. Afterward, I went between my cousin's house and home. It was weird. My level of understanding of anything was mute. I was confused and angry. I wanted to cry and scream, but letting go scared me. I was afraid that I would be lost in a dark, desperate place forever if I finally let go. I really didn't want people at school to know what had happened. I remember feeling embarrassed and self-conscious. My dad kept me off school for weeks. I couldn't sleep at night. I would creep downstairs, and my dad would be asleep on the couch. My older sister and I would cook, clean, and try to take care of our younger sister. My dad took us food shopping, but none of us knew what to get. Most days, we would go up to the cemetery with my dad. We would also go up alone. People tried to get me to talk. But I didn't want to talk to anyone. I was scared to speak, scared to let go. It was over a month before I went back to school. On my first day back at school, I met my friend; she told me that our form tutor had told everyone what had happened. That my mum had died suddenly. I was so mad. I knew it was not her fault and couldn't be angry at her. I just felt sick and walked to school with dread. Walking into school was weird. All these people that I rarely spoke with came up to me. Patting my hair, telling me I was pretty, that my shoes were nice. Like, what the fuck! I just pushed past and walked into my form room. My friends there were different. They just let me be. I sank into my desk, got all my class assignments, and continued my day. The school was like that for a while. In the end, I just ignored people. I didn't know what classes I was supposed to be in or where I was supposed to be. I flitted around until lunch, then skipped to the woods for a smoke. I rarely went back to school after lunch. I would bug the smart boys to copy their work, get the homework assignments, etc., and they always did. They were my rocks, and they never knew it. School life was like this: showing up when I could, staying for a few lessons, and leaving. I couldn't focus on anything. My younger sister and I would go to my aunt's after school. She would make us tea and marmite sandwiches. We would stay an hour or so and then usually walk home. One time I walked straight home from school, I was in my own head thinking about nothing and everything. There was a block of garages that I took a shortcut through, it would bring me out right across from our house. As I turned out of the garages, I suddenly stopped. My house was there, but it looked different. A breath escaped me as I realized my Mum was dead. She was not sitting in the back garden drinking tea with her friends, she was not at home waiting for me to not tell her about my day. How had I forgotten this? I felt like a brick wall had just crushed me. These moments of my mind forgetting seemed to protect me from the reality of pain. But when my mind accepted the truth the freshness of it, crushed me.

Life was becoming routine; it was hushed and lonely. People wanted me to open up and talk. But I was too scared too. My mind and mouth were blocked, and I couldn't speak, even if I wanted to. I went to my family doctor one time. He asked how I was. "Fine!"

"Do you miss your mum?"

"NO!"

My eyes welled with tears, and my body became hot, cold, and clammy. I could not speak or hear anything else. He told me to come back anytime I needed to talk. I never did. One morning at school was tough, and I desperately wanted to go to the cemetery. I asked a friend to go with me. We walked up. It was not close, and it took ages to get there. I looked at my mum's headstone. I began to break down. I started screaming and clawing at the soil, trying to get to her. My knees sank in the wet grass and mud, and my hands were covered in mud. I just started sobbing. I had never broken down that way before; I quickly composed myself and stopped. The tears and mud on my face were streaming. My friend helped me to my feet. We hugged and left. Walking back, she started singing silly songs. We linked arms and sang silly songs all the way back. I felt a moment of reprieve. I could breathe for a few minutes. This friend saved me that day.

FOUR
PRUNING SHEARS

What gives a young child the intuition to flee a trusted adult when feelings become unsafe? A betrayal of innocence, taking advantage of a vulnerable child. How does the child summon the courage to run?

It was November of 1983. My mum had died just 6 weeks before, and I had just started to go back to school. Being 13, I was definitely into the top 40, pop music and top of the pops. We lived in a small town just north of London, so to have a pop concert there was very rare. But we heard that a famous singer was coming to our small concert hall. Everyone was really excited. My dad and his friend got some tickets, and we all went. It was my dad, his friend and daughters, my sister and I. The hall was large and dark and we were standing at the back. I wanted to distance myself from the adults, so as to feel more grown up. I moved away a bit and stood alone, listening to the music and taking in the concert setting. My dad's friend came and stood behind me. He started asking me questions, I think about the concert. I am not sure what I mumbled, but I moved away. Again, he came and stood behind me, really close so I could feel his body and his breathing down my neck. I felt discomfort, disgust and shock. My mind was buzzing and racing, I couldn't concentrate on the music. My stomach was both nauseous and burning. I kept walking away; he kept following and continuing to stand right against me. I glanced to where my dad and sister were. They were at the back of the hall amongst only a scattering of people. I walked away again and tried to get lost in the music, when he followed and stood next to me pushing his shoulder into mine. He asked was I enjoying the concert. His breath smelled stale and damp. I made my way back to my dad, who was not enjoying himself. My younger sister was standing next to my dad and swaying her head to the music. I saw the friends' daughters standing away from us all. They were watching the show and singing along. I really didn't know what was happening, only that it shouldn't be happening to me. I felt self-conscious, weird and icky. My mind couldn't think properly or keep track of my surroundings and time. I really just wanted the night to end. I went and stood at the back by my dad and I felt relief as the concert slowed down and came to an end. I kept thinking what I had done wrong to make this happen? What actually did happen? Did I do something to make that happen? I was so confused about the entire evening. It was the first of many times I felt confused and uncertain of situations involving this person.

Not long after this I was at their house talking about a gym routine I had been practicing. The husband wanted me to show it to him. We put a Madonna record on, and I did a few flips, twirls, and somersaults. He looked interested and said I should go on. I did a bit more, he was so creepy standing there, telling me which parts he liked the most and that I should do them again. He looked weird and I felt uncomfortable and cold, but also sad that he didn't like the second part. I said, "No, I am done."

It was weird, he wanted to see more but we were all ready to play outside, he tried to make me stay and do it again. I felt odd at this, but brushed it off. He particularly disliked that me and the youngest daughter would spend all our time playing board games, and listening to pop music in her bedroom. He would stand outside her door telling me I had to come down. He wanted me to sit on the couch watching TV rather than playing. He would sit next to me, talk about his hobbies and things, and ask me how school was and what I liked to do. It was always just me; everyone else could go and play. It was like he was trying to be my friend; it was bizarre. His wife, my mum's friend, would be in the kitchen making dinner; I would try any excuse not to go over there without my dad.

They would invite me and my sisters over for Saturdays or dinner. Her husband continued to sit on the couch with me, talking like we were friends, challenging my knowledge and laughing at me. He was a bit weird; their house smelled funny, and I always felt uncomfortable and really self-conscious while there. One day, their youngest daughter told me I had changed; I didn't smile with my eyes anymore. I just shrugged; what could I say? What did I have to smile about?

One Saturday, their eldest daughter asked me to go upstairs to her room; it smelled like makeup and hairspray. I felt grown up and privileged. She then wanted me to go into the parent's bedroom. Parents' bedrooms were always a bit taboo and I felt super weird and uncomfortable. I was shown some pics of women in underwear, she told me she liked to pretend to be like them. It was a bit bizarre as she stripped and lay on the bed. I was told to do the same. I felt sick and frozen to the spot; my heart started to beat fast. I heard noises and footsteps on the stairs; I jumped down the side of the bed and hid. I was terrified. The dad came in and looked at his daughter sprawled half-naked on the bed. It freaked me out. I was hiding under sheets on the floor, totally frozen in fear. When he left, I was told I had ruined everything by hiding. I just wanted to vomit. They turned quite nasty. I believe I ran downstairs and ran home. I wanted to tell someone, but I wasn't even sure what had happened. It was all so strange.

That same Summer, our two families all went on holiday together. If I remember, it was a caravan site close to the seaside. My younger sister and I slept on the pull-out couches in the living room area. The husband told us we had to get undressed, put on our jammies, and not be shy while he stood there watching. It made me feel self-conscious and embarrassed, so I always tried to hide when I changed.

On the beach, we were playing on the sand and in the sea. I remember laying on the towel, feeling the sun's warmth. I was trying to get warmed up before running down and jumping into the waves. The husband came and sat next to me, so close it felt prickly; he would be leering at me, telling me it was hot out and I should take my shirt off. I felt sick and terrified. I was frozen, unable to move. His face was so close I could smell his sweat. It made me feel sick. His wife was next to him. She turned and said, quite sternly and nastily, "Just take it off and get it over with."

I don't remember my reaction. I could not move. I just lay there, frozen, willing myself not to jump up and claw his eyes out. I ignored them and eventually, they moved away a bit; I could finally jump up and run into the sea. That week was awful. I didn't want to go anywhere or eat anything; I felt sick the entire time and relieved when it was time to go home. We never went away with them again, and as far as I can remember, I never again went to their house.

FIVE
STEP-PARENT TYRANNY

Abusive step-parents can worsen a grieving child's pain. Emotional turmoil deepens wounds and intensifies the longing for maternal love and guidance.

PART 1 Madame Grimhilde

***A** year or so after my mum died, things were becoming rough at home; my dad had moved a girlfriend in who was physically and verbally abusive to us all. Not only my younger sister and I, but also her two small children. My dad was still wrapped in grief but was trying to move on.*

My Dad had been very sad and lonely since our Mum died. My sisters and I agreed he should try and meet someone. My dad's mum set my dad up on a date with a friend of a friend who knew someone similar to my dad's age. This woman had an older child, older than me, and two small children. She seemed friendly, and they went out for dinner. They came home and looked quite happy. We were excited to see my dad happy. Maybe a month or so later, my dad said she was coming for a visit with her two smaller children. We all thought it was just a visit and got busy cleaning the house. She arrived with too many suitcases for a few days; we found out that the girlfriend was actually moving in with her kids. It was quite a shock; my sisters and I were all taken aback by this new situation. Very quickly after the girlfriend moved in, things began to change. Beforehand, I would spend my days listening to music, trying to keep up with my schoolwork, I also had a weekend job at the local sweet shop. I went to the cemetery most Sundays with my dad. I didn't want to talk about my mum; it was too physically painful, and those last words I spoke to her tortured me. I would spend time at my mum's sister's or cousin's house. Once the girlfriend moved in, my family thought things would improve. A stepmum, support, and a loving family home again. It was nothing like that. The girlfriend ripped the wallpaper off my bedroom walls, and her kids were given bunk beds in my room, which I was okay with, but I had lost my safe space. She took the fridge and all the food; she then stored them in their bedroom and put a lock on the door. If we wanted to eat, we had to ask permission. Usually, all we got was a lot of verbal abuse. My sisters and I had to clean up after them constantly, and it was never good enough, so we had to do it repeatedly. The girlfriend would fire verbal abuse at us, rip our clothes, and throw them out. She would pinch me in the back and upper arms, grab my upper arm, and squeeze it while whispering nasty abuse in my ears, pulling my hair, calling me names. I tried to set up a homework area in the dining room but couldn't, as it was for eating. I tried to sit in the living room, but it was always too noisy, and I wasn't allowed to sit on the couches. She would walk across my work and rip the papers. With my dad, she was always sweet. Made him lovely dinners and acted nice to everyone. I did try to stay behind in the school library after school, but my dad decided I had to come home right after school. I tried talking to my aunt and cousins about the situation, but nothing happened. They told me I had to get used to the new situation and give the girlfriend a chance. She was nice and was trying hard! No one seemed to believe what was happening. I became so angry and would often yell my anger out. This girlfriend was being physically and verbally abusive to us all, and we had to suck it up and like her. The girlfriend's eldest son would stay in his room and smoke pot all day. I tried to get along with him; sometimes it was okay and other times he would spit at us, slam doors, punch holes in the wall or mumble meanness under his breath.

My dad took his girlfriend on holiday one time, and my dad's mum stayed with us. It was lovely having my nan stay with us. She was funny and loving, I could relax and breathe a bit. One particular night, my nan made a nice dinner for us all. We were all in the kitchen cleaning up after dinner. The eldest boy came in and spat all over the clean dishes. It was disgusting, and my nan told him that. He reared up and started to yell at my nan. Calling her all kinds of disgusting names. I was so angry that I started to yell at him, too. He turned on me and started to push me and call me names. I grabbed a fork and tried to stab him in the hand. I was so angry; all the years of loss and abuse were welling up in me. I wanted to hurt him and hurt him badly. He backed away and left. My nan was so upset. My younger sister took her to the other room while I cleaned and scrubbed dishes.

I was in my last year of high school and desperately wanted to do well in my exams, which was weird as I rarely spent an entire day in school. I would stay up late, read over my work, and copy the homework assignments. I couldn't do this while anyone was awake. I would sneak out of my window at night and go walking. Scamming a neighbor to grab me a bottle of cheap wine to drink. I did talk to my form tutor about life at home. I opened up to him about some of the abuse. He wanted to talk to my dad, but I was terrified of the backlash, so I pleaded with him not to. My dad was in a bad place at this time; he was lost and angry, and I didn't want to upset the boat any more than necessary. It did feel good to talk to someone, though. I still couldn't talk about my mum. I had a block, and words would never come. It made me feel dizzy, hot, and nauseous. Those last words I spoke to her would echo in my mind.

I also felt very disconnected from my friends. Not being allowed to stay after school or see my friends outside of school isolated me. The school even spoke about separating me from my one good friend at school. We would link arms and walk around the school. The support we gave to each other was enormous. I would go to her house when allowed, and she showed me how to do my hair and dress nicely. The hairbrush and toiletries at home were also locked away; my clothes kept getting torn or disappearing. We were not allowed to have nice things. As final exam time was approaching, my dad's girlfriend would allow me to study with friends. One friend I studied with had such lovely parents; her mum would bring food to us while we worked. We would hang out at hers, study, and eat. Then, head into town, or the boyfriends would pop by. It was nice to have some normality. I had to run home, though, fear of being late pumped my adrenaline to a sprint. Her parents were normal to me, though she would complain so much about her mum. Things like, "My mum doesn't understand me, she doesn't let me do what I want, she tells me I have to be home at a particular time, won't buy me these clothes."

These conversations would occur often; I didn't say much and tried not to listen. I attempted a few times to say something, but it was hard. Complaining about her mum, I just turned to her and said, "You are lucky you have a mum."

Actually, I think I yelled it. She just stopped, looked at me, I ran. I couldn't keep myself together. Our friendship ended, and I couldn't cope any longer. The summer came, my dad often worked late, especially over the weekends, so I didn't see him so much. The girlfriend was always there. She would go through my stuff, throw or destroy things, and continued her tirade of verbal abuse. It was like I couldn't escape her; wherever I was in the house I would find her standing behind me. She had stopped hurting me by this time, as I started to push back physically. My younger sister and her own two small children were constantly in trouble and getting punished for reasons that were very unclear. I would hear the verbal insults she flew at them and saw the bruises and welts left behind. I felt powerless to help. The anger inside me was scary. I just wanted my mum back and things to go back to normal. My family would barely talk to me; I was so tired, angry and sad that I was making questionable decisions. My dad's parents always had time for me; they had moved close by, and I spent a lot of time there, I mean a lot! Any spare time I had; I would walk over to them. Sitting with my Nan was like it always had been. We laughed, made up silly jokes, and watched old movies. She would put old pieces of foam down to make a bed in the sitting room. I never had to ask. It was the only place I felt welcome and at home. I tried to talk to my mum's sister about the situation, but it seemed exaggerated; I was told to accept things. No one seemed to believe me and often would lose their patience with my complaining. I began to feel distanced from them all. As soon as I was sixteen and had left school, I left home. Leaving my little sister in that house was devastatingly hard, but I needed to escape for my sanity. I foolishly trusted that my family would step in and help. I felt like I needed a fresh start, to break away and move forward on my own. I wanted to leave my baggage behind, shed my skin, and try on a new me. I found a tiny bedsit; I told my dad a few days before because I was scared of what the girlfriend would do. I badly didn't want to leave my younger sister in that situation, but I knew that if I didn't go, I would probably do something I regretted. I packed all my belongings in plastic grocery bags, my dad called me a taxi. He hugged me and told me I would always have a home there. I had not had a home there for several years. I held my breath and left.

PART 2 Madame Tremaine

I moved to the city and began working as a live-in nanny, taking college classes during the day and after work. I worked evenings and weekends, anything to keep myself and my mind occupied. I moved a lot, I would leave whenever I felt too comfortable or familiar with a situation, always feeling like if I stayed too long, they would find out; what I didn't know, it just made me uncomfortable to stay too long. I made new friends; being teens and young adults, we would all get up to stupid shit, often verging on dangerous. I would step back and walk away. I didn't want people to know or see me; I didn't want to get too close to anyone. I feared being rejected and hurt.

I spent a lot of weekends with my dad's mum, I loved my nan so much. She was funny and kind and always had something mischievous up her sleeve. She was my person, the person I felt free and safe with. My nan was one of the only people in my family with whom I still had a relationship; I didn't feel judged or that I had ever let her down. I was just trying to move forward and forge a new life for myself, but it felt that every time I gained a step, I would fall back fifty. My nan told me she was cut off from my little sister and would try to call and see her when the girlfriend or her kids were not around.

A year went by, and my dad was now living with a new girlfriend; she had two kids around my age. I felt uncomfortable around them; they snickered and made snide, behind-the-hand comments. I would try to go home every month or so, it was never good. The new girlfriend was unfriendly and mostly ignored me. In the evenings, I would stay and chat with my younger sister, who wasn't allowed out until she had finished everyone's laundry, ironed, cleaned up all the dishes, and tidied up the house. It made my heart ache, the things they made her do. She told me once that she felt like Cinderella but knew there was no fairy godmother coming to rescue her. This girlfriend's kids were spiteful and would say untruthful things about me, my mum, and my sisters while I was within earshot. It was like they were talking with each other, but loud enough so I could hear; they would spread lies to my friends and family. I thought it was pathetic and childish. Of the many things I endured from Dad's girlfriend and her kids, one thing stands out: knowing how hard Mum's passing had hit us, they took the opportunity to inform me and my sisters that our aunty (Mum's sister) and our cousins had told them we were forgotten. The girlfriend and her kids were now seen as a family, and Mum's memory, my sisters, and myself were all no longer relevant within the family. On one visit, I was staying with my dad and his girlfriend, I had arranged to meet my cousin for lunch. I ran to her house, excited for a lovely catch-up and chat. There was no answer at the door. I waited longer than I should have, hoping she was running late. Disappointed, I took myself for a walk and think by the river. I didn't want to head back to the house and have the girlfriend mock me for my cousin standing me up. I walked over to my aunt's house to see if anyone was home. My cousin was there, they both looked at me and asked where I had been, they had been waiting hours for me. I didn't understand what was going on, I went to my cousins at the time she had said. I found out that the night before, my cousin had called my dad's girlfriend; she asked her to tell me the plan for lunch had changed and to meet her somewhere else. Of course, she didn't mention it to me at all. I told them this, unsure if they would believe me or not. I felt like I had let them down and disappointed them again. Why couldn't I get my life right? Later that night when I went back to the house, the girlfriend asked if I had a good day and what I did. I saw a look in her eyes. I didn't want her to feel like she had won, so I responded, "I had a lovely visit with my cousin, thanks."

I would take the bus back home every few weekends when I could wrangle some days off. I rarely saw my dad; whether he wanted to see me or was too busy with work was hit-and-miss. I went to see my mum's sister, but it was also strained. It felt like I was a visitor and not family. My mum's sister once confronted me and asked me how I could have left my younger sister in that situation and that I should have protected her. I couldn't believe what I was hearing. In disbelief, I told her, not so nicely, that I was sixteen when I left, that she, as my mum's sister, should have stepped in and protected all of us. I felt overwhelmed with anger and sadness. Why couldn't they see the truth for what it was? My mum and her sister, my aunt, were so close that I felt she would look out for us. But she was dealing with her grief and sadness differently, and I only saw mine.

I was allowed to move back into my childhood home one summer. It was strange. I was sleeping in my childhood bedroom, which I had left only three and a half years before, but it felt alien. There was nothing of me here. Nothing of my mum here. My mum's photos were gone, as though she never existed. The only photos I remember seeing were of the girlfriends' children. I didn't care so much; nothing surprised me anymore. The girlfriend's kids were planning a vacation abroad. One of them couldn't go, as she was pregnant, and my dad's girlfriend asked me if I could take her place. I imagined going on holiday with them and their friends, it took me half a breath to say thanks but no thanks. The screaming and yelling that came at me, calling me a selfish bitch, saying I was just like my mother. Seriously, and you think this will make me go even more. No way. I was forced to lend out my suitcase, though I had just bought a new one. It was returned to me with what looked like a knife slash right across the front. I found it stashed under the stairs days after their return. It was still full of stinky, unwashed clothes. I dumped them where they were and cleaned up my suitcase. It stank and was filthy. Dad's girlfriend's kid came by a few days later; the rank clothes were still where I put them; I was making tea for my dad. I heard her scream, "What the hell is this? Who did this?"

She came into the kitchen, punched me in my back, grabbed the back of my hair and yanked. My dad came in and asked what was going on. "This bitch dumped all my stuff everywhere; I'm going to fucking kill her," she started swinging at me again. She was a lot bigger and heavier than me.

I backed up and said, "It's my suitcase; you should have cleaned your shit out of it, and by the way, why is it slashed?"

My dad told her to leave, and she did. Then he told me he had accidentally slashed the case while picking her up from the airport. I believe this as much as I believe the sun and the moon are the same planet. I stayed away as much as I could, they had seemed to me to have built a family unit, and I wasn't welcomed, so why bother?

Five years later, my younger sister got married. I had moved to Canada and was engaged by this time. She decided to get married in the registry office in town. My fiancé and I flew over for the wedding. The night before her wedding, my older sister and I wanted to spend time with her to catch up, support her on this new adventure, hold her hand, giggle, hug and do everything sisters do. We called the house. My dad's girlfriend answered the phone; my sister was staying with them the night before her wedding. We were told that our younger sister was not feeling well, wanted to be alone, and had already gone to bed. In other words, do not come over. My older sister had a little stubborn rage. "We are going over; I don't care what she says."

I was a bit nervous; this girlfriend had a mean streak and could be intimidating. We didn't even knock; we just flew open the door and marched in. Our younger sister was sitting on the couch, my dad was reading the newspaper, and the TV was droning on. She jumped up and ran over to hug us. She had thought we were not coming to see her. She told us that Dad's girlfriend had called us to come over and we replied that we had other plans and were going out. My younger sister said she was devastated; all she wanted was for us to come over. She asked us, "What made you change your minds?"

We all held each other and cried. How could someone who was a mother themselves want three sisters who had no mother, do something like this? It was hatred and jealousy in its purest form. We went down to the registry office early to see her arrive. To our surprise they were already in the registry office. We were thirty minutes early, how could they be starting already? I suspected we were given the wrong time to be there. We walked in and the registrar said no more people; the room was packed. Like hell it is. My little sister is getting married, and we are staying, those people can leave! I pointed at the girlfriend's kids and told them, not so politely, to get out. I was so mad I could barely think straight. The two daughters shot me with evil looks, put a smug face on, and left. Watching my sister get married was a wonderful moment. I was so proud of her. She had endured so much, I wanted nothing but good things and happiness for her. The rest of the wedding was as much a shambles as the evening before and morning was. I felt like anything the girlfriend and daughters could do to prevent us from attending, they did. We were three hours late for the reception due to the girlfriend not booking the car for us, as she had promised. When Steve and I walked in, I saw her evil smile and wanted to smack her into next year. I ignored her though and hugged my younger sister. She was all I cared about.

We stayed away from my dad and his girlfriend for the rest of the visit. Steve flew back to Canada, and I spent Christmas with my older sister and niece for the first time in almost ten years. It was a magical day.

My dad decided to get married a few months later: He didn't tell us. Why, I don't know. I cared too little about them and their lives; it hardly registered for me. The abuse from this girlfriend was not physical, but it was just as harmful: She alienated me from my family. The pattern of emotional and familial alienation abuse continued for as long as she was involved with my dad.

SIX
ACROSS THE POND

Leaving England, I was full of grief and sadness. I needed a change, a fresh beginning. I wanted an adventure and a life that was my own.

When I was nineteen, I applied for a job in Canada before my younger sister got married. I needed a fresh start, a place to begin again and reinvent myself. It felt like all I was doing in England was running from one disaster to another, and I wanted it to stop. It took several months to get a job, work permits, and immigration status. During that time, I went back to my dad's house. I had been away for three and a half years but felt like a stranger walking into my family home. It was strange. My dad was now with someone new. The abusive girlfriend was finally gone, and I hoped things were going to be better. They were not; this new girlfriend was very jealous. She had two kids the same age as us and always pitted us against them. I found it childish and would not go along with her games. My younger sister was not so lucky. I'd found a job in Canada, booked my flight, and was ready for my next adventure.

I made a few new friends. There were a few English

girls in the neighborhood. We all went out one Saturday, and I was introduced to Steve. We met almost four months after I arrived. We became fast friends. He made me laugh so hard. Our little gang of friends would go into the city on weekends. We trolled the malls and ended up in the nightclubs. Steve would come by during the week, and we would go for coffee and donuts! He helped me find a better job, and our friendship grew. We became very close friends and eventually began dating properly. Steve was from a strong Italian Catholic family. I was a bit weary of his family. I found it hard to trust them – families, that is. His family seemed so normal to me. His mum would cook these huge dinners, and his parents' Italian accents were so thick it took a while for me to understand them. I felt shy and inferior around them. I didn't want them to know too much about me. Was I ashamed? Maybe? I think I was more embarrassed that I perceived myself as unlovable to my family than actually ashamed of my family. If they knew I felt isolated and rejected by my family, then I wouldn't be worthy. I did open up to Steve gradually; he was supportive and understanding. I could talk to him so openly and without fear. I took Steve to visit England. I was a bit nervous, as it was also my first time back since leaving. It was wonderful seeing my sisters again. We chatted and caught up; it was like a bond of love that held us together.

The next time I went to England, I went alone. My mum's dad had died. My mum now had both her parents with her. This gave me a little comfort, but I was also losing so much connection to my mum. My tears came hot and steady. My heart was breaking again. I stayed at my granddad's house with my aunt. We went through old photos and Grandad's possessions. I found his old tobacco tin. The scent brought back a million memories. I took home his bear that my nana had made. He had slept with it for many years. It was a reminder of both of my mum's parents. I went to see him at the funeral home; I wanted to put red-scented roses in his coffin. Those were his favorites. Standing there, looking at him, I froze. The feeling of fear and wanting to hug him were overwhelming. I put the roses around him, prayed and told him I loved him.

Arriving back in Canada, I was quiet and didn't want to talk about it much. The fear of speaking about my grief and feelings was overwhelming. I knew if I let go, it would be messy. The feelings of missing my mum and losing my grandfather were all messy and tangled up. One Sunday, Steve and I were out driving. I started to tremble. My body felt like it was going to explode; the pain was so intense that I could barely breathe. Steve pulled over and I just melted. Melted into a heap of intense pain and hot tears. It was ten years since my mum was ripped from me, those last words to her haunting me. My body and mind were screaming. Steve just held me. Put his arms around me. I could feel the safety and love of his hold as my body and mind screamed. I don't know what triggered this; I was completely drained. It was the first time I could let go and feel my pain; I felt safe with Steve. I felt his love for all my good and ugly bits.

Steve and I began to plan our wedding for the following summer. We had just returned from my younger sister's wedding and had a lot to plan. He wanted a church wedding; growing up catholic and attending church every week, this made a lot of sense. For reasons that were unclear to me I agreed to a church wedding, but not a catholic one. We settled on Anglican. I asked my dad to come, to give me away. He said he couldn't afford it. We offered to pay; he said he would think about it. Then he was too busy. I am not sure if I was more angry or sad at this. My dad's parents, brother, and family all came to my wedding, just not my dad. My dad's dad, my grandpop gave me away, and my young cousins were my bridesmaids. Looking around my wedding, I barely knew anyone; these were all Steve's family, his friends, who were now our friends, but where was I here? I didn't recognize the person I was; it all seemed unreal. I was a different person who had left England five years prior; I felt like an imposter. I took my husband's name. I didn't want to. I tried to remain myself and keep my identity as my mother's daughter. Who would I be if I wasn't her daughter? Steve, being from a strong, completely faithful traditional family, felt it was important I took his last name. The first time I said my new name, saw it printed, and wrote it down, I felt like I had come home. It fitted me like a warm sweater I could curl up in and fell off my lips like a creamy dessert. My old name made me feel uncomfortable and itchy, like a shirt that was too tight around the shoulders and didn't button up without a gap. I felt safe. I could stop running, sit, and breathe.

Steve and I bought a house. A lovely bungalow in a small neighborhood just outside of the city. For the first year, it was so echoey and bare: we barely had enough furniture to fill it. We used bedsheets for window coverings. Our weekends were full of painting and shopping for furniture and kitchen appliances. When we weren't doing this, we would take day and weekend trips to explore our province, fish, and hike. He would take his mum to church on the weekends, and we often had dinner at her house. She would make so much food we could eat leftovers for the rest of the week! We were building a home and family. Within two years of getting married, we welcomed our first child. We had both wished on a shooting star while driving one night. Unknown to each other, we had wished for the same thing:

a child. The new baby brought so much joy and connectedness to us. I was building my family, and we were going to be strong. Steve held our new baby before I did. I remember watching him as he looked into his child's eyes. It was mesmerizing, pure love and pride. I could tell he would fight dragons for this baby.

SEVEN

FROM MOTHERLESS DAUGHTER TO MOTHERLESS MOTHER

Navigating motherhood without my own mum added a layer of complexity requiring resilience and strength. Enduring abuse from the (step) mums deepened my resolve to create a nurturing environment for my own growing family.

I found motherhood challenging. How was I supposed to know how to mother when I didn't have one? I missed her so much. I wanted her to meet her grandchildren. I wanted mothering experience, advice, and criticism. I wanted a mum. I wanted my mum. I would cry most days, just missing her. The pain of not having my mum around as I became a mum was brutal. My mind would scream out for her all the time. There was one moment when I was breastfeeding my first baby. I had welcome baby cards on the top of a cabinet. I was praying hard for my mum, to feel her, to have her hold me. I was so tired and low I couldn't cope. Something from the top of the cabinet came down. It was a card. The words on the front of the card were about being a wonderful Mum, welcome to motherhood, or something along those lines. It felt like a sign that she was close and watching over me. Without her, the thought of raising children and being a mum was scary. I missed her so much; the chats, sage advice, parenting conflicts, and everything we should have gone through together. My head would spin in despair; I felt desperate to reach out. I missed something I never had, and I missed it with every ounce of my body.

Within a year, we were expecting again. The moment I told Steve, he spoke our unborn child's name. It was like he already knew our baby. Our second child was born; what a difference being a parent of two under two was. The role of parenthood enthralled me. It was busy, messy, and a bit overwhelming; I rarely got dressed on the days Steve worked. He would come home from work and take the kids to the swings every day, popping them in the stroller or our blue wagon and trundling down the streets. This gave me time to shower, clean up, and cook dinner. I was like a freaking fireball getting everything done before they returned. We took them camping that first summer when our second was born. Our old tent was cold and damp, so we upgraded to a small tent trailer. The first morning we woke up, my eldest lifted his little hand, scratched the side of the trailer, and said, "I love Camping."

Our baby was only a few months old, so we had a carry sling that first year. And would take long hikes along the trails and play in the lakes. We took them fishing on the boat in the late afternoons. It was so peaceful bobbing along the lake, watching the sunset.

Our third baby ended in a miscarriage. It was devastating. It was a bit of a surprise pregnancy, and we both felt we had bitten off more than we could handle with a third. But when it ended, we both realized how much we wanted it. The night we lost our baby was awful. Steve bathed and put the kids to bed. He was torn between helping me and making sure our kids were okay. I became very unstable after this. I was anxious to be pregnant again, I could feel the emptiness inside my body; it was a void I needed to fill. I felt like I had, in some way, failed this little one, that I was not good enough to be its mother. I prayed so hard for my lost baby to find peace in heaven. I bought a small ceramic ornament of a baby sleeping on a cloud. The words inscribed were "safe in the arms of Jesus". I cried in the store when I saw this; I held onto it and put it next to my bed. I would pray that my unborn baby was safe and in heaven. A few of my friends were also pregnant at this time, I couldn't bear to be around them; I would duck behind counters at the grocery store if I saw them. I was so sad, so, so sad.

I did get pregnant again, only a few months later. It was a scary pregnancy; I feared losing this little one almost every day. This beautiful little family of mine was almost complete. Life was tough and stressful, having small children. I stayed home with them and tried giving them as much of me as possible. During my third pregnancy, I decided to get Christened on the same day as my two older children. We had started to attend our local Anglican church; it had a wonderful, supportive family atmosphere. I felt that God had surrounded me with faith and trust. Guided me, held my hand throughout my life, and showed me the way. I found strength in prayer and knowing He had not rejected me; it was a profound moment for me. I felt brave and honored to call myself a Christian.

My rainbow baby was born the day before my nan's birthday. She was thrilled. But also disappointed that I didn't hold my breath for another thirty minutes! She wanted a great-grandchild on her birthday. This was as close as she was going to get! I had my rainbow baby. This little one made my family complete. I would wrap my family up in strength and softness and not let anyone or anything hurt us. Steve and I rested in bed after our youngest was born; our midwives cleaned up and left. Our bedroom door flew open, and our middle child bounced in like Tigger. "Shh. be careful; the baby is here," I whispered.

My toddler stopped mid-bounce and said, "The baby's here, can I see?"

I gently pulled the blanket back, my bouncy child touched the baby's cheek, and gently leaned over and planted a sweet kiss. Our eldest came in, stroked the baby's head, and said, "Hello, little baby."

We all snuggled up. There were four toddler hands gently touching our newborn. They were in awe.

As a family, we did everything possible for our kids: sporting events, art classes, swimming lessons. It felt like we were constantly on the way somewhere. Steve was so proud of his kids. He wanted to give them every single experience possible. We hiked, camped, fished, went to carnival fairgrounds, and visited family. We cut our own fresh Christmas tree every year. It was important for us to build traditions and memories that would continue for a lifetime. Cutting down our Christmas tree was a family event. Each year, I would search for a different Christmas tree farm to visit. There were definite prerequisites we required. A few varieties of Christmas trees, wagon rides, hot chocolate, and of course, Santa. We would listen to Christmas music on the way up to the farm. For the first several years, we always met up with a 2nd cousin of mine and his family. I discovered a few years after moving here that my mum's uncle had moved to Canada when he was a young man and raised a family here as well. I was not very close to them and did not see them much, but the eldest had married, and I was quite close to his wife, and their child and my children felt like cousins. Once at the farm, we would jump on the wagon, some were horse-drawn, others tractor-drawn. It was always a bumpy road towards the Christmas trees. Once we found a good spot, the kids would run through the trees trying to find that perfect tree for Christmas. It was usually very cold and snowy, I loved watching them run through the Christmas tree forest with snowsuits, snow boots, and toques. Finding that one tree was so exciting. The kids would all lay on their bellies and take turns with Steve, helping him saw the tree down. Then it was time for Santa, hot chocolate, and treats. It was only a few years ago when my eldest, and their partner, both in their mid-twenties, all went together to pick and chop down our Christmas tree. It was one of those full-cycle moments that lifted my heart.

The kids and Steve loved camping. Our small tent trailer became our home for much of the summer. The parks we visited had large natural lakes, hiking trails, and rocky and sandy beaches. We took the kid's bikes, and they would ride around the dirt path at the campground for hours. Steve taught them how to chop wood, build fires, put worms on fishing hooks, and identify poison ivy and other not-so-friendly plants. We took night walks with flashlights, shining the lights through the dark wooded areas that always looked so spooky. One evening, I was putting the two little ones to bed. Steve was outside with our eldest. I could hear them chatter. "Look, Daddy, a dog."

Steve was like, "Omg! Don't move,"

"But it's a dog, Daddy."

"Don't move," was all I could hear Steve say. I peeked out and saw, by the light of the campfire, a skunk standing between them. The two of them were still as rocks until the skunk sauntered away. Steve scooped up our eldest and brought him in. He was laughing so hard. That could have been a very stinky night. We often camped in early Summer and Fall when the mornings were still a little cool, and we could see our breath. We would build a small fire and make a pot of coffee and hot chocolate. The kids would sit around the fire, as the morning sky was brightening, in their jammies, sweaters, and wellie boots, sipping a large mug of hot chocolate. I can still see them sitting in the large camping chairs with their little legs in yellow wellies swinging back and forth. We would be planning our adventures for the day. We would hike trails through beaver ponds, glacial erratic rocks, and go searching for snakes, both land and water snakes! Search trails for animal footprints and poop! And fish, the kids and Steve loved to fish. On boats, off docks, in the middle of streams. One time, we were fishing in a small swampy lake area. One of the kids was reeling in what seemed like a huge catch. As it emerged from the water, we heard a scream, "It's a monster!"

They had caught a large catfish, and they do look pretty monster-like. We also rented cottages during the summers; we could take our boat then. We always rented places right on lakes. The kids would run down the dock and jump into the lakes. We had a firm rule though: life jackets were to be worn at all times. We had an inflatable tube that we pulled along the back of the boat. The kids loved it as we sped up in the lake, and they bounced up and down, crashing on the waves. We also had a kayak. The kids could go out alone and explore the freshwater marshes, pretending to be Huckleberry Finn or Phileas Fogg! We would hang the life jackets on trees each night to dry off and watch the stars appear in the sky and the lake turn to inky blackness. On one trip, our youngest kept asking about the life jackets hanging on the trees. They wanted to know what it felt like.

Eventually, we gave in; I zipped them up in their yellow dinosaur life jacket, with the little red ropey hook at the back, and hung it from the tree. It looked so funny, hanging there, little pudgy toddler legs swinging six feet in the air. We took a picture; they were giggling and waving. When I took them down, I asked if they wanted to do it again another day. "Not really," was the reply.

Our last big family holiday was to Florida, Disney World. We took the trip with Steve's sister and her family. It was spring, but still very hot there. We rented a large condominium, and we all bunked in together. On our first day there, we went to the Lego store in Downtown Disney, of course. My eldest loved Lego, and it was a must! They had huge Lego statues, a Lego Loch Ness monster in the river, and a store with more Lego than you can ever imagine. Our youngest found a stationary Harley bike, so Steve and the kids all took a seat and posed! It was a very hot and memorable family holiday. We visited all the parks posed with Buzz, Mickey, and Minnie Mouse, Rafiki, Pocahontas, Stitch, and Daisy Duck. Our youngest was being such a jokester with Stitch that he took his blue fluffy paws and covered their faces up. They loved Goofy, and while with Buzz Lightyear, Zurg captured them and put them all in jail! The rides were fun, they couldn't get enough and we nipped into the cooling zone, where they had cool water spraying. Driving back and forth to the theme parks, we saw these random people selling Alligator jerky from their cars. As tempting as it was, we declined to try it. We drove to Kennedy Space Center, there were thousands of bugs splattering on our car, and not even the window washer could keep up. Apparently, they were love bugs; I definitely didn't love them; with the heat, they seemed to petrify themselves to the hot car. The space center was very impressive. We took the full guided tour, and Steve and our eldest were particularly impressed. The two youngest were more interested in watching the alligators in the pond. During our trip, the kids were excited to visit the Animal Kingdom. Our eldest woke up not feeling so good. Me being a great mum, I told him to suck it up. Which, like a champ, they did. Until about fifteen minutes after we entered the park. It was obvious this was not going to be a good day, so my brother-in-law drove them back to the condo. They missed out on such a great day; it made my heart sad. When we returned, they said they had slept most of the day and felt a bit better. We do believe it was a bit of food poisoning that only they got. Apparently, there were some wild strawberries on the roadside that were probably eaten and maybe shouldn't have been. There was a pool in the condo area, the kids would all strip down and jump in when we arrived back. The cooling effect soothed some hotheads and frustrations. We flew back to Buffalo airport, picked up our car, and crossed the border to come home. It was after midnight, and we were all very tired. The three kids in the back were wearing Mickey's hands, Goofy hats, and Disney shirts and were all catching flies. The customs officer looked at them and laughed. We were there for only a week but left with a million memories.

EIGHT
MELANOMA

Being diagnosed with cancer is devastating. As a family we made a commitment to face this together and have the courage and strength to walk this path with grace and faith.

Our youngest was barely a toddler when I found Steve sitting alone in the basement one day. He had his shirt off, which was very unusual. I noticed a tiny mole on his chest. It was the size of a pencil eraser, perfectly round and black. It startled me. I asked him how long he had that for. He had noticed it a month or so before. I asked him to get it checked out by his doctor. I had to nag him for months to get it checked. He finally told me the doctor said it looked fine, but another one on his back looked a little weird. He was to make an appointment for removal. He got three moles removed several weeks later. His Dr called and told him to make an appointment with the specialist at his clinic to discuss the results. Another six weeks went by. At the appointment, this specialist told us he didn't understand why we were there. We should have been referred to an oncologist. What! Yes! The little black mole that his doctor was not concerned about was malignant melanoma. Steve had cancer. We were spinning. My heart was thumping so loud in my ears that I started to panic. I need to take control and see what the next steps are. The specialist told us he could not do the referral; only the primary care doctor could. He was not there that day. I started to yell. I made a scene so bad that the nurses called the doctor's home to send the referral in as soon as possible. Steve's primary care doctor had never encountered Malignant Melanoma before, so he didn't know the protocol. He promised to deal with it. Steve needs a wide incision of the original site and a sentinel node biopsy. They needed to check they had all the cancer and see if any had spread into his lymph nodes. We needed to get this surgery done as soon as possible. We needed to remove any remaining cancer and start treatment. We hit a snag, though. Our city was going through a Sars epidemic. All the hospitals were dealing with emergencies only, surgeries were being canceled, and they could not guarantee or schedule surgery. I started calling other provinces in Canada. They would not take anyone from here for fear of spreading Sars. I even called some private hospitals in the States. I would pay with everything I had for this surgery. He couldn't start any treatment until he had it, and we were already two months behind the starting line. I called the main hospital's cancer clinic every single day. I knew all the medical receptionists by name. I knew the best time to call to get a surgery date booked. I called every single morning and afternoon for weeks. Finally, a surgeon had a spot available. He was a breast cancer surgeon, but the surgery was the same. We had a date. It was only a few days away, and we did not have time to plan much, but we did. The kids would stay over at a friend's, and I would drop Steve off and sit outside the hospital until it was over. I couldn't go inside due to the epidemic. The morning of the surgery came. We were getting ready to leave when I got a call. Apparently, a woman had been diagnosed with advanced breast cancer and needed the surgery urgently. Would it be okay to reschedule? I wanted to scream, "No, what about us?" But there was something telling me we should do this. We agreed to reschedule for a few days later. The surgery took pretty much all day. I sat outside the hospital and waited. The surgeon called and told me what time to pick up. I watched through the glass doors as they wheeled him to the entranceway. I was parked in the turn-around waiting area. Something happened, and the doctors and nurses were surrounding him, and he was whisked away again. I started tapping on the window to find out what was happening. Apparently, Steve woke up pretty hungry after surgery. Instead of soup, he wanted fried chicken. Fried chicken! After major surgery. I felt a bit bad for him, but seriously, he kind of deserved to throw up at that point. The surgery went well; all the margins were clear. It was protocol after melanoma surgery, and at that time, to start interferon once healed; this meant having shots every day for a month, then once a week for as long as tolerated, ideally for a year. The treatment was rough on Steve. He would be holed up in bed, shivering, the day after each treatment. He told me it was like being hit with the worst flu every week. He could not eat these days, and he basically looked like hell. He wanted to do the treatment as long as possible and would work in the days between the treatments. He told me staying home would make him overthink. He continued to take the kids to their sporting events. Those times gave him so much joy. He felt like shit, was freezing all the time, but was so proud to watch his kids. They gave him all his joy. One day, just after he came home, he told me he felt superhuman. Yeah right! You are on weekly chemo and feel like crap, but you are not letting it stop you; I think you are superhuman. I hugged him. But he said no, this is different. He lay down on the couch. I was watching him; he seemed to be relaxed but was also staring intently. "Am I running around the house right now?"

What?! "No! You are lying on the couch."

He told me he felt like he was running around the house. On his way home from work, he got stuck in traffic; he said he felt like he could pick up his car and run home. Alarm bells were ringing in my head. He continued, "I knew I could do it, but I also knew it wasn't what people did."

This really concerned me. I called the nurse agency, as he was supposed to get his needle that day. We agreed to hold off. I got in touch with his oncologist's nurse, who agreed not to continue the needles at this point. Steve was heartbroken. He badly wanted to complete the year; we were at the almost 11-month mark. A visit with his oncologist confirmed that Steve was having an adverse reaction and it was not safe to continue. His blood work looked good; stats were good. After a few weeks, he felt tons better, and life got back to a pretty normal pace. He had scans and blood work quite frequently. Always looked good. We began to relax and breathe again. The kids were growing. We were busy parents; between sports, camping, and fishing, life became pretty normal again. I put the horror of the past two years behind me. This was not going to touch me.

NINE
I'M A GNU

The loss of my nan who had been my guiding light, a constant source of love and strength, left a gaping hole in my heart. It's as if a part of myself had been torn away, forever leaving a void with echoes of memories, unwavering presence, and love.

As a child, my dad's mum, my nan, was a huge person in my life. She had big red curly hair, which she usually held in a pink chiffon head scarf. I thought she was so flashy and glamorous. She always had a tube of pink lipstick in her bag that she would dot on her cheek, rub in like blush, and smear across her lips. Then, she'd open her compact and powder her nose. My nan's closet was full of flashy costume jewelry, clip-on earrings, and endless pairs of shoes each with a matching outfit. Her dresser was full of glass bottles of different perfumes. I remember vividly watching her spray White Linen on each side of her neck down her chest, she's swooped her arm across her face, spraying perfume all over her face and hair. Then, with a giggle, she would put a little squirt behind her, on her tush. I would run my hands through the beads of her necklaces and bury my face in her dress suits. I actually think there were as many, still with their tags on, as not. She would tell me she needed outfits for when she lost and gained weight. My nan was on a perpetual diet; she would only eat one apple because they had too many points, but when we went out, she would treat us to fresh cream buns. Custard creams or digestive biscuits with our cup of tea, and always, Rum raisin ice cream late at night. She would tell me that eating this ice cream was a secret because it was supposed to be for grown-ups only! I would pretend I liked this ice cream; it always tasted a bit bitter, and honestly, raisins have no business being in ice cream. Rum or no rum!

My nan's favourite color was green, but everything about her was pink. She had this pink bathroom with what I thought was the longest pink bathtub ever. I could lay down, head to toe, in my nans' tub and still have room to slide around. She had these big puffy balls in tubs of talcum powder and a doll with a pink crochet skirt that sat on top of her toilet paper. It wasn't called toilet paper, though; my nan called it bum fudder! After my bath, I would puff my entire body with the talcum powder, put my jammies on, and wrap myself in her fluffy pink bathrobe. I would stand on my tip toes and jump up by the sink, trying to peek into the bathroom mirror to comb my hair. There was always a rude joke on the edge of my nan's lips. We visited a stately home once, and this young lad walked by wearing jodhpurs. I was maybe ten years old at the time. My Nan said, "Look, it's like two little eggs in a hankie."

I had no idea what she meant, but she was laughing so hard that I began to laugh as well. These one-liners she made up, she repeated for years after, always with a wink and a giggle. My dad had dropped me off at hers for a school term break once when I was around nine or ten, I was feeling a bit cool, so she went upstairs and got me a jumper from Granddad's drawer. When he came home later that day, we were watching TV; he poked his head around the door to say hello. He looked at me, "I've got a jumper just like that," he said. My nan and I howled with laughter. He just looked at us, shook his head, and left.

We would often catch the bus or train and take long walks in the surrounding parks and villages. My nan would tell me stories about the Bronte sisters. There was a time when I was young when I thought the Bronte sisters and my nan were friends; she had so many stories about them and would tell me secrets that they had apparently told her as well. My nan's imagination and love held no limits. We had been pen-pals since I was a small child. She had taken me to the zoo once when I was much younger, and we came across this large animal with a huge nose. We didn't know what it was and tried to guess; a deer, a moose, or a deer/donkey. After about ten minutes of watching this funny animal stroll about, we saw a sign on the wall. "I'm a gnu," it said. My nan and I set about laughing so hard. We repeated those words: "I'm a Gnu, I'm a Gnu."

I really don't know why we thought it was so funny, but it was. From then on, whenever we wrote to each other, we put a little poem in it. "I'm a gnu, a gnu, and you have a smelly toot!"

When my youngest was about three years old, I took them all to England. Steve couldn't get any time off work, and he wanted to save his vacation days to take us all camping. We visited my dad's mum, my nan, who had long since moved back north. Watching her play and joke around with my children filled my heart with joy. I recognized then that my nan, although not my bio nan, had been sent to me. She was the mother I had missed for so many years. She guided me, advised me, understood me, told me off, held me, and loved my children, all in the same way my mum would have. I felt blessed to have this beautiful, funny lady in my life. My memories of time with my nan will be cherished forever. We talked about Steve's cancer. My nan told me that she had survived melanoma, and so would he. I was grateful for her trust and faith in the universe. We took the kids to the zoo; my nan had a motorized bike chair type of thing that we had rented. We were given explicit instructions; the kids were not allowed on. Every moment no one was looking, my nan would call the kids over and give them rides on it. She kept getting caught by the zoo staff and told off. "Okay, sir, sorry, I didn't know..."

As soon as they were out of sight, "Quick, get on, while no one is looking!!"

I looked at her and my kids. They were laughing together, conspiring together, making up silly songs together. I loved her with all my bits and pieces, and she loved my kids. My heart was happy.

Not long after our return, my nan wasn't doing so well. She was in a lot of pain and couldn't move very much. I tried to call her as much as I could. I would write silly messages and send them. She called me one day; she was being taken to the hospital. I was relieved and scared at the same time. My first instinct was to fly over and visit. It was tough with the three boys, though. Steve could only do so much on his own, we were a busy family. I called the hospital and begged the ward nurses to let me speak with her. She sounded soft and frail; she sounded scared. As we talked, she told me she had seen her sisters/brothers, who had long passed. She had seen her grandchild who passed away as a two-year-old baby, but he was now a grown man and very handsome! She told me she was going to die soon, I told her not to be so silly. I needed to hear her crack her funny jokes, be rude about the people around her, and be sassy about the nurses. She sounded quiet and very tired. I wanted to go to England and be with my nan, I wanted to crawl into bed with her, hold her close, feel her body, and love embrace me, give her all the love she had given me. I needed this so desperately. I was discouraged to go, that if I showed up, she would know that she was dying. I was so fucking mad about that, I wanted to hold my nan in my arms and tell her how much she meant to me, but I wasn't allowed because she would think she was dying! I couldn't get my head around that logic. My kids were watching me crumble on my bed and crying. Steve came home from work. He told me to do what I needed to do. I cleaned up my teary snotty face and made the decision to book a flight. Almost, almost at the same moment, my phone rang. It was my sister. She was crying. Nan's gone. The floor swallowed me up. I was holding my breath, not wanting to feel the pain. The pain I felt when I lost my mum. I knew I would not survive that pain again. The intensity of the pain didn't come though; it was as though my body had remembered the journey, and I knew I was going to be okay. I just felt a loss, a deep hole of sadness in my heart. Steve took charge and put me on a plane.

I stayed with my dad's brother. He took me to see her. She looked so tiny. I don't remember her being so tiny. She was always this huge personality to me. Looking so small and vulnerable didn't seem right. My grandfather also looked tiny. I saw him sitting on the couch in my uncle's house. His head was down, he was shaking his head in disbelief. They had been together since the end of WWII; it was a lifetime. I grabbed him and gave him a huge hug. He started crying. I had never seen him cry. He looked so sad and crumpled. We went over to their flat; my dad and younger sister were there also. It was obvious to me that rummaging of my nan's belongings had already begun. My younger sister showed me a bunch of letters next to my nan's chair. They were from me. She had kept my letters; she had sat in her chair and read and re-read all the words and love I had poured into those letters. My nan had sent me things of hers over the years, her pearl choker necklace, to wear on my wedding day. Which I did and still do on occasion. She had sent me a fluffy pink scarf that she wore when I was a child. It was always so soft and warm that I used to beg her to let me wear it. It had arrived one day, all packaged up for me. She had sent a note. "I'm a Gnu, I'm a Gnu, to keep you warm, I'm sending my love to you," love Nan.

I went into the bathroom, opened the bathroom cabinet, and saw my nan's face compact. She was always powdering her nose. I opened it; it had a mirror inside. I brought it to my face and breathed in the scent. Closing my eyes, I could feel my nan. The softness of her. I breathed in her scent and could feel her all around me. I asked my grandfather if I could have this. I tucked it in my pocket. To this day, I often open the compact and close my eyes. The scent of her surrounds me.

At the funeral home, I pinned a Mother of Mary brooch on my nan's blouse. I tucked one of my letters in, kissed her cheek, and said, "I'm a Gnu, I'm a Gnu, and for always, I'm going to miss you."

Saying goodbye to my nan was one of the hardest things I had experienced. She was my safety, my person, my other mum. I didn't know how to be me without my nan, I didn't know how to be, period.

I only stayed for the week. Steve picked me up from the

airport with our three kids in the back of the car. He had dressed them all up in their English footy gear. I had missed them so much, but I was also in a bit of shock from the funeral. Getting home, Steve had them all so organized. They all ran to their rooms, packed their school bags for the next day, and organized their own clothes. It was too funny to see. He had the house and kid's ship shape. I think he loved being a solo dad for the week. The kids all looked so happy. This was my life; this was my family. Our life moved on, as it does.

TEN

RETURN OF THE BEAST

When cancer rears its ugly head again, it grips you with an incomprehensible fear. Those moments leading up to test results are filled with hope and dread. Yet amongst the turmoil, you find a resolve to stay strong and face whatever comes with courage and determination.

Steve regularly visited his oncologist for scans, blood, and mole mapping. He really liked the oncology surgeon he saw; Steve would go to the breast clinic to see him every few months. He always giggled when he came home, as the clinic had a sitting room feel and had pictures and models of breasts all over. He, of course, was the only guy there. He was doing well; he started cycling; he had a road bike and an off-road bike and would cycle around 15-20 kms several times a week. We had a fishing boat; he would take the kids fishing as often as possible. As our eldest got older, he didn't want to go so much, and the youngest was too little to supervise alone, so unless I went, it was just Steve and our middle one. We had spoken to the boys about melanoma, and at the time of Steve's first surgery, they were aware of the importance of sun protection. Though they knew the importance of it and their dad's battle, life was moving on, and I, for one, didn't want to dwell on our cancer saga. Even thinking about it made me panic. I would see kids and other parents with sunburns over the summers, and I felt nauseous. Each of my kids had a high-spectrum sun cream on them at all times. I often thought that others thought I was overreacting a bit, that I was being a bit anal. But it played on my mind all the time. Steve was also cautious; he wore sun protection at all times, and he had changed his diet to an "anti-cancer" diet. Organic meats, no dairy, no sugar, etc. Steve was determined not to hear the C word again.

A few years went by, the kids grew, and we enjoyed all the usual family of five adventures and stresses. We really were just an average, boring family. We camped a lot. Steve taught the kids to build campfires, pitch tents, build shelters, and fish. We rented cottages on lakes; we took the boys water tubing and lake diving. As a kid and teen, he was into dirt bikes and had bought a mini dirt bike and fixed it up. We would take it to the cottages, and the kids would ride around on it. We spent a lot of time at his mum's house. She had a huge backyard, and they often rode the mini bike around it. We built a tire swing in her backyard, and these kids had hours of fun on it. In our own backyard, Steve had built a treehouse against an old oak tree we had. This was not a prefab store-bought tree house. He had designed and built this one himself. It had a huge wavy slide for the kids to scoot down. Every winter, once the deep freeze set in, He would build an ice rink in the back. Building solid boards for the sides and spending hours flooding the frozen ground, smoothing, and making it even. Flooding, smoothing again and again until he had a solid layer of ice for the kids to skate on. The kids' friends would come over and play shinny hockey. Often late at night, after dinner, we would put the backyard lights on, and the kids would skate until exhausted for bed. We went to family movie nights, sports tournaments, conservation areas in all seasons, and beach days. We did all we could do, with rarely a spare day. It was great. Steve and I didn't feel a need to get away from the kids, we enjoyed our life with them. We even went to hotels with mini-golf and play pools for weekends to have a mini break away, but all together. Just a normal, young, busy family.

Steve came up to me one night, a few years after he finished his first cancer treatment. He wanted me to feel a lump he found in his armpit. I felt it and almost threw up. He said, "It's bad, isn't it?"

What could I say? I am not a medical professional. He called his oncologist and got a quick appointment a few days later. It was early afternoon, so he went straight from work, and we would meet at home. The doctor had aspirated the lump, and Steve said all he could see was black liquid filling up the syringe! We know Melanoma tumors are black, and even though it still had to be tested, Steve knew what that meant.

The labs came back positive for Melanoma, and a surgery was scheduled. He would be having the tumor and all the lymph nodes removed from the area. We tried to give the boys just enough information that we felt they could handle. Trying to deal with what this actually meant for us and keeping our lives as normal as possible was so hard. I felt like I was torn between grief, fear, being goofy with the kids, and a rock for Steve. I felt like someone was actually laughing at me, saying, "Ha, and you thought you could live happily ever after!"

Steve's mum was coming to the hospital with us and then back to stay with the kids. When the surgeon came to take him in, his blood pressure was sky-high, and they called me in to try and calm and reassure him. They would not do surgery with such high pressure. He looked terrified; he told me he thought he was going to die in surgery. I told him, not to be silly, that I needed way too much help with the kids right now. I reassured him that we loved him, and everything was going to be fine.

I hated this, I hated seeing my strong husband be so sick and vulnerable, I hated the journey we were on. This was not supposed to happen. I breathed deeply, straightening myself, adjusting my crown, putting on a fake strength, and told myself, I can do this, I have to do this, I have no choice.

Steve had all his lymph nodes removed in that arm. The Melanoma tumor had overtaken, almost eaten the nodes. He now had to be careful with infections. He would wear latex gloves while shopping, working on the car, putting gas in the car; anything that required him to touch things that other people had touched. He started radiation therapy and chemotherapy. For his radiation, he had little tattoo marks on his chest. He would show the kids and say, "Look, Dad's a tough guy!"

At one appointment, I had to take one of the kids to an adjoining hospital for some tests. We were at hospitals across the street from each other. The porters walked us through all the underground passages that connected them. I was exhausted, running between the two. But these two were fine, it was a day out for them. I could tell the kids were scared. Our youngest had really never known a time when their dad was not dealing with this; our eldest was turning into a stroppy pre-teen, as they do. And our middle, who was Dad's shadow, began to retreat. It broke my heart again and again to keep them updated on what was happening. We could come home on the bus after treatments, and the kids would be doing their homework, bugging us for food, destroying the house with Lego. Steve and I would go to our room, take a breath, hold each other for a moment, and go out into the chaos of parenting. I desperately tried to hold things together, terrified. Our kids had questions, so many questions. They wanted to know what our oncologist was like, was he going to fix everything, was he nice. We arranged for them to come to visit, so they could meet his Dr. They were very shy walking around the big glass corridors in the hospital. At home, they had a million questions, but here, they just looked wide-eyed and small. I held their hands and said they could ask me questions any time and I would pass them along, and that there was a donut shop downstairs we could go to afterward. Being a responsible parent, a terrified wife, and not wanting to see our children go through this was hard. I wanted to scream and run away every day. I wanted to rip this bloody cancer out and kick it into hell. I wanted to crumble into a ball and disappear. I wasn't allowed to though, I had to stay light and funny, smile, make jokes, pretend. Pretend. I feared so deeply that our kids would go through that ripping pain that I had experienced. I had no blueprint to follow as a parent and a wife, I had my sisters and a few friends to confide in, but I needed my mum, I needed my nan, I needed my person, and my person was sick.

Once chemo started, it became like a date day for Steve and I. We had to be there early in the morning for blood work, then wait and come back a few hours later for the treatment. We would stroll around downtown, go for lunch, window shop, and visit Chinatown to pick up his green tea leaves, turmeric root, and other remedies he was taking in the hopes of winning. Sometimes, we would forget why we were there; it seemed so normal to browse around, holding hands and finding hidden gems of food places tucked away. I was aware of the time though, and as the clock ticked closer to heading back to the hospital, my heart would start racing. I could also see it in Steve's eyes. I don't think we ever said anything, we just turned and headed back to the hospital. Chemo daycare was tucked away at the top of the hospital. We would arrive and see if his meds were ready, sitting there waiting was torture. I would look around at all the other people waiting. It was always so quiet. As I looked around one day, I took note of the people there. There was a young man, a teenager really. He was lying on a hospital trolly bed. He looked so tiny and pale; what I assumed were his parents were sitting with him; his dad kept his head low while his mum kept her hand on his back. It was like she didn't want to let go, as long as she could touch him, he was still here. I saw a young mum; she was in a wheelchair with a baby strapped to her on one side, and she had her infusion on the other. This peaceful calm room held so much sadness and despair. I would get Steve settled in the chemo chair and then pop down to the coffee shop to pick up coffee and muffins. One time, when I came back up, they had flipped his chair right back, his feet were pointing to the ceiling, and several nurses were working on him. It was a scary moment for me. I watched as they took his stats and re-did the chemo port, blood pressure, and everything. I walked over and said jokingly, "What the Hell are you up to now, Steve?" he looked pale and out of it. The nurses told me that something had happened with the flow of the chemo, it was entering too fast or something. Steve had passed out, and his heart rate went crazy. I didn't realize how serious this was at the time. I always tried to make light of the situation, keep a smile on my face and a quirk in my talk. It was tough, I felt like two different people. It was lonely. We did get through the chemo and radiotherapy, Steve had appointments every other week. Oncologists, dermatologists, scans, blood. His diary was filled up; he would book these days off work as vacation days and work extra hours to compensate. I didn't know how he did all of this. He was so very strong, and I admired his determination. He wanted to live and would do whatever it took. He would tell me, it scared him, that he wished the kids didn't have to go through all of this. It was so unfair. We always tried to put it behind us and move on. The beast was chasing us though.

I watched him one early spring day, the ice rink was melting, and he was taking down the boards to let the ice melt and flow. This ordinarily would take him less than an hour. He was outside all afternoon. Sitting on the little ice-skate stool. I asked him what was up. He said he was so tired that he didn't have any energy left. He looked so pale. I tried to put this to the back of my mind, to ignore the obvious signs. He had finished chemo almost a year back, he should be feeling good.

It was PA Day, the kids were off school, and a group of us were all going bowling. There were a bunch of kids and their mums in my driveway. My phone rang, we were running late, so I wanted to ignore it. Something told me no; I had answered this call. The kids' eyes all rolled at me! It was Steve's family Dr. He told me Steve had done bloods that day, and he needed him immediately to get a transfusion. Steve was at work. He refused a pickup and insisted on driving home. The Dr wanted me ready, in the car, to drive Steve straight to the hospital. My friends saw the look of horror on my face grabbed the kids and left with them. I felt sick waiting for him. He shows up all relaxed, wanting a snack and shower. Like wtf! I mentioned his Dr had called, and we were to go right now. This surprised him. I had to drive, as per the doctor. On the way to the hospital, Steve said, "You know, I don't think this cancer is gonna kill me; I think something else will."

I looked at him and replied, "Can you promise me that?'

At the hospital, they saw us right away and had his blood ready. I sat on this broken plastic chair for seven hours while Steve got his transfusion. He told me it was like eating a good steak! He began to feel better already. My ass was so sore sitting on the broken chair, so I crawled onto the hospital bed, and we both took a nap. My friends took the kids for the day, fed them, and put them to bed. When we got home, I snuck into the basement bathroom and called my older sister. I was such a mess, I couldn't talk. I was just breaking down. This hell was not going to end. We had appointments with the Drs later that week. They had to find out the cause of the blood loss. They wanted to do a colonoscopy to see what was going on. I wanted more scans and MRIs. The colonoscopy was booked several months away. I was not happy, so I got on the phone and insisted on proper scans. Like yesterday. I actually lost it on the doctor; I knew this rodeo; I knew what needed to happen. The scans were not good. He was scheduled for surgery again. They were going to open him up and get as much as they could. He would have to stay in hospital for several weeks following this. This surgery was long, it took almost all day, and in recovery he was in so much pain. They gave him a pain pump, but he was too unaware of it. His mum was with me. I drove her back to stay with the kids, and I settled down in the hospital for the night. He could not walk without lots of pain, but would shuffle down the corridor every day. I admired his determination. The kids drew him pictures, which I put up in his room. I was working full-time, had to get the kids to school, home, dinner, after-school activities and back to the hospital. It was almost three weeks before he came home. The kids were so happy to see him, he had changed though, he had lost a lot of weight, his pain level was increasing, he was pale, tired all the time, and his frustration level was quite high, he was fed up. He just wanted to feel better and get on with things. Once he had somewhat healed from the surgery, we went for scans to see what was going on. It was not good news. The cancer was spreading, they were small invasive aliens creating havoc in his body. His liver, lungs, and omentum – the lining of his stomach, and his optic nerve. I couldn't even look at the screen as the Dr showed us the scans. I knew all we had now was time. Steve nudged me to look. Did he know? He was always so optimistic like he really believed he would win. This Dr told us there was nothing more he could do. That we had just a few months. He got us back in touch with our original oncologist, he was running clinical trials. We went home with a plan. We had exhausted all conventional therapies. It was up to science now. We walked into the house and collapsed on the bed. Steve asked me to tell the kids. He couldn't face telling them. I decided to speak with the kids individually, they were all different ages and levels of understanding. I tried to explain that the cancer had spread throughout Dad's body, and we were going to try new treatments, and clinical trials, to hopefully shrink the tumors, stabilize the cancer, and stop more spreading, but how do you tell them this was it? I had visions of when my dad picked me up from my neighbor's house, and I asked where my mum was. That answer of "everything is going to be alright" gave me false hope. It was a hope I desperately needed, but I now know that I needed the truth; but the truth is hard and ugly. Our eldest, being a young teenager, understood more than our youngest. Teens always seem to know so much, so much more than parents can give them credit for. Our eldest was getting older and desperate to gain autonomy. I remembered how I was at that age, I was a shit, thought my parents knew nothing, and they annoyed and embarrassed me constantly. I also realized I was my eldest's age when I said those last awful words to my mum. I realized it was my age, my time between childhood and adulthood, which caused those unforgivable hurtful words. The words were not real, they didn't reflect my feelings. I saw our eldest child, going through that same period of growing up. It was going to be tough. Our middle was his dad's shadow, a mini-me. Ever since Steve said our middle one's name, as soon as I told him I was pregnant again, they were like one person. I could see the rip, the shredded hole that was going to be left. Our baby, now only seven years old, had barely a chance to have a healthy dad. Steve started to get sick, not long after our youngest was born. Would Steve be remembered as the strong, caring, funny loving dad, in our youngest's eyes, or would he be a shadow of a memory? My heart broke for my children, my heart broke for myself. I curled up in bed one night, the fear and hopelessness gripped me. My heart was racing, I felt nauseous, dizzy, and hopeless. I could not go through this again, the pain was unbearable. I wanted to run, every cell in my body was screaming to run. I wanted to strap myself and my kids inside our car and disappear from this world forever.

I had always run before, cut ties, and started again, leaving the destruction behind. I went to church that weekend, and after the service, I fell to my knees and prayed, praying that I could find something to hold on to. I could not do this anymore. Please, God, help me.

I could not run though, I had to stay and fight, fight with Steve, and fight for our kids. Our future was running out of time, Steve wanted to live, and I had to fight his fight, next to him.

The clinical trials were rough; he had to go through endless tests just to see if he qualified and read and sign pages and pages of documents. Most of the treatments were in pill form, we were able to take them at home. The side effects were rough though. Steve insisted on working, through all of this, I also worked full time, and the kids still had their after-school sports to go to. We had to go for bloods and scans every couple of weeks. We began to use the days downtown as date days again. Meeting up for lunch, taking some much-needed alone time. That hour, life seemed so normal, it felt great to reconnect and feel normal. Our walk to the hospital felt like the green mile as fear and dread would creep in. Waiting to see the Dr. after the tests was gut-wrenching. One time, our regular oncologist was away, we had a visiting Dr, he was nice. He looked over Steve's current medications and supplements. He asked Steve why he was taking a particular drug; it was for cholesterol. He told him he didn't need to take that one anymore; Steve was confused, "Is my cholesterol okay now?"

"Well, no, not really, you just don't have to worry about that anymore," alarm bells rang in my head, and Steve looked confused. I looked at the doctor; I knew what he was saying; how was I going to tell Steve he probably wasn't going to live long enough to worry about high cholesterol?

His labs came back okay that day, we could breathe for a minute. It felt like a small reprieve, we had another two weeks of clinical trials with this drug. The tumors had stabilized, which is good news for today. It always felt like those days were the only days we could breathe. If there was growth or spread in the tumors, we had to start again, look for a new clinical trial, go through the qualifying tests, and paperwork, and pray for approval. At one point, it looked so good, the tumors in his lungs were practically invisible, and the liver ones were shrinking. This was the best result we'd had. We felt like we had won this battle, that in a few more weeks he would be NED (no evidence of disease) that is the most that anyone with stage 4 cancer can hope for.

When we went back a few weeks later, our trial nurse started to remove Steve's port, but she didn't say anything. We were like, whoa, we need this, what are you doing? She told us the Dr would be in soon, and that the scans showed some growth. We went into one of those family rooms and waited for the Dr. Steve was tired and laid on the bed. I curled up behind him, and we both fell asleep for a few minutes. The Dr came in, actually, several doctors and nurses came in the room, this was not good. They told us, the tumors had pretty much exploded all over his body, there were spots in his brain now, we had exhausted all treatments and trials. One nurse looked at Steve and said "You have a wonderful loving strong wife with you.

I piped up, wanting to lighten this black mood, "Me? I am only here for the insurance money!"

Steve nudged me, giggled, and told me to be serious for a moment.

He was still working! His Dr said, no, you cannot work anymore. Steve protested, he liked working, he wanted to provide for his family, and it kept his mind away from reality. He was told he had to stop, no driving, no work. He did not want to leave that day, leaving the hospital for the last time meant giving up, Steve was not ready to give up.

ELEVEN
THE DAY I LEARNED TO PUMP GAS

Once again, learning to rise from the ashes was exhausting. This time, though, I had my children to look out for. To keep them from falling, I had to stand taller and straighter than I possibly felt I had the strength to. I had to move from darkness to light.

Steve literally did everything for me. Even on cold, blizzardy days, he would take both our cars to the gas station to fuel up. I knew I needed to learn how to do this myself. Standing there, at the gas station I saw my life change. Everything I had fought for, all my traveled roads, had led me here. My husband was going to die, I was going to be a widow, a single mum, my kids were going to have their lives torn apart, and it was just me. I couldn't run; I had to stay and try to glue these pieces back together. I stood there, at the gas station, and my life had changed instantly. Steve was amazing though; he made all his plans. Called the financial guys, the insurance guys, and got in touch with human resources at work. He spoke with our priest. He had dotted as many I's and crossed as many T's as possible. I got in touch with services that could help our kids. I wanted them to have some kind of therapy, someone to talk to. They each were such different kids, their therapy had to reflect this.

We went on our last camping trip. We visited our favorite campground. The kids did all the work setting up the tents, the lanterns, rope lines, and getting the firepit organized. The years he had spent taking them camping and showing them how to do stuff had paid off. We were close to a small beach and lake, and we spent a lot of time there. Steve would spend hours sitting on the rocks, staring at the lake. The kids cooked all the meals and cleaned up. This really was just hot dogs, burgers, bagged salad, snack chips, and, of course, Smores! Steve had given up on his anti-cancer diet, he just wanted to eat what he enjoyed, so we did. Evenings were spent sitting around the campfire, talking, and not talking, late into the night. It was so peaceful at night. The sky was so dark, the stars so bright and present, the firebugs would fly and glow in and out of sight. All we could hear were the clawing, rubbing, whining, and clicking sounds of the night creatures; the waves of the lake moving against the rocks. It was like time was standing still, I could have lived in that moment forever. Our kids played sports, the eldest had played on the same footy team for nearly eight years. They were in a competitive league, and this Summer, they were in the championship finals. Steve really wanted to go. Sitting in a car, and being up for long, at this point, was really tough on him. We got to the field just before kick-off, and Steve decided to walk up to the top of the stands, I tried to get him to sit at the bottom, but he was being stubborn. The other parents all said hi to Steve, and as we sat and watched the game, I noticed that the dads shimmied closer to us, very discreetly. It was a great first half, their team was doing amazing. At the end of the first half, Steve went to stand up. I stood up quickly in front of him, scared he would fall face first down the stand stairs. All of a sudden, like out of nowhere it seemed, the dads were all there. It was so discreet and respectful that they held onto him, chatting, goofing around, getting him slowly down the stairs, keeping his balance in check. I felt the strength and love in that moment. Steve was in a lot of pain, he wanted to go home, on our drive back one of the mums called, she had our eldest on the phone. Steve heard that they had won the championship game. He put a stupid grin on his face all the way home. The parents of the footy team all got together and sent us away to an indoor water park and hotel for a long weekend. They had arranged early check-in, late check-out, and a large ground-floor suite. It was such a precious gift of family time and memory-making they had gifted us. The kids loved the water park, so many activities for them, Steve and I floated around and around the lazy river. It was a great weekend, we ate at the buffet, watched movies at night, my youngest snuggled up with Dad, and they both slept in each other's love.

Steve was looking very thin, pale, and sick at this point, I tried to ignore the glances, the stares of pity, and the look-backs, but it was hard. He looked obviously sick. We had popped into Walmart one time, he told me he looked rough, even for Walmart. I told him, he was the handsomest man in Walmart that day! We had to laugh! I have seen this look on several people since, and it sets my heart racing on fire. The look of someone actively dying, trying to live, is so devastating.

I gave up work. Life was not easy. Day by day, hour by hour Steve's pain increased, and the pain meds were not helping. We bought a wheelchair and hospital bed into the house. One of his childhood friends came by, and he took Steve out for a walk in the wheelchair. He bought beers and pizza, as that's what the two of them had done for over thirty years. Steve was unable to swallow food well by this time, and I would hold liquids in a straw and empty them into his mouth. He was not going to be able to drink beer or eat pizza, but he was happy holding the beer can on his lap, his understanding was vague, but something told him that beer was good! Steve became more and more confused, and his anxiety was interfering with his sleep. We would get him settled in bed, with cushions and blankets to make him as comfortable as possible. I would rub his back and hair, to ease him into sleep, then quietly slip out. Almost instantly, he would be up, and following me down the hallway. He became very sick one night and I drove him to the ER. Being in palliative care they took us in right away, he had a blood transfusion and a catheter fitted. On our way home, several hours later, he told me, no more. He didn't want any more hospital visits. Just to stay home. My two sisters flew over. Steve looked at my younger sister and said, "It's you!"

He reached out and held her hand. My mind reeled at this moment. Just a week before, Steve had been lying in bed. He told me that he wasn't sure if he was dreaming or not, but it felt real. He saw a woman's face, looking down at him, she looked peaceful and was talking to him, but not out loud, like talking in his mind. He said he felt peace, that this person was either going to help him cross over or who he would be in his next life. I believe, at the moment Steve said, "It's you," he was looking at the person he had seen, and it was my younger sister. The tumor on his stomach was so huge, his body emaciated, with a ten-month pregnant-looking belly. I could see the outlines of the tumors. He wanted me to rub his tummy, but I couldn't. The thought of touching the tumors made me physically ill. I had a good friend who spent a lot of time with us, at that time, she would sit for hours, rubbing his belly. His mum would come by and spend hours rubbing his feet. I was barely holding things together, I would try to keep a normal house, making breakfast, getting the kids to school, homework, laundry, and then I would feel the ground fall beneath me as I spun into a pit of anxiety and despair. As quickly as I fell, I straightened back up. I couldn't fall apart; I had three kids to stop from falling apart. I needed to be stronger, stronger than I felt or wanted to be.

Steve refused to lie down. He would be pacing around for hours. The Dr came and told him it was okay to lie down and rest. I wrapped my arms around him, hugged and kissed him, and told him to rest and sleep. He turned to everyone there, my sisters, kids, Dr, and hugged everyone. I went back in for a second hug, he looked at me and said, "I already hugged you."

He didn't know me. I looked into his gorgeous blue eyes and saw nothing.

Steve died on the last day of September; he was forty-two. My mum had died on the first day of September, so many years before, she was thirty-six. Our children were the same ages as me and my sisters were when our mum died. Life can be cruel like that.

I was a mess; I went between breaking down and having to stand tall. I couldn't stand to be at home, it felt so empty and echoey, that I wanted to hide. The kids were struggling, I thought I was strong enough to help them, but I wasn't. I faked strength, I faked smiles, I was faking life. The kids were unhappy, school was stressful for them, and they fought at home all the time. I switched their bedrooms around to help relieve stress and reconnect them. We were all so bubbled up in grief though, we couldn't see each other. I had a few people I could talk to, but they seemed to want so much from me. I wanted to talk about things when I wanted, and not, when I didn't. I seemed fine one day, and a disaster the other. I could not manage my job anymore, I went back to work a month after Steve passed, it was fine for a few weeks, but then I lost focus, my concentration was shot. I was tired all the time. I quit; I couldn't cope, I needed to be present for my kids, and right now I had nothing. I thought being at home, having more time with the kids, and by myself would help. I couldn't focus, I didn't want to be alone, and I didn't want to be around people. I felt itchy and irritated in my own skin. I didn't want to be home; I couldn't cope to be away. I felt stuck in fight or flight mode. After a few months at home, I signed up for some college computer courses. My thinking was to keep my brain busy. I felt restless at home, I couldn't concentrate during the class. The teachers' words sounded like the mumblings of the teacher in Charlie Brown. The computer screen was a jumble of knots. I would stay behind most days, to get some clarity, and untangle my confusion. My middle was in therapy, and we had family therapy once in a while, it would often leave my brain until the last minute, and then I would be rushing to attend. I wasn't coping well; I was uncomfortable in my own skin. Trying to be strong for your kids, when you are falling apart is hard. It's like trying to glue a flat puzzle upright; pieces kept falling and disappearing. I tried to use my experience to help my kids. To tell them that I had been there, in that dark hole, and had managed to climb out. I would look back on my climb though, and be reminded how messy and destructive it was. I wanted better for my kids. I just didn't know how to do it. I was failing miserably.

TWELVE
ONE FOOT IN FRONT OF THE OTHER

Learning to love again, is not leaving behind the ones you loved and lost, it's forging a new path, acknowledging the hurt, but refusing to let it define you. Have the courage to step forward into the unknown. With your heart intact.

I met a guy who had lost his wife to the same cancer as Steve, many years before. He could understand the conflict of emotions I was going through. We would talk for hours sometimes. Just having him there, someone who understood, who I could talk to about real things, the messy parts, the wanting to run away, the need to stand and fight. The act of grieving someone whilst they are still alive, watching your whole world die in one corner, and in the other corner, you are making dinner and taking the kids to school. I could escape into this net of understanding and just be me. After some time, we started to date a bit. That was conflicting; how do you let someone new in your life when your entire world was ripped from you? You can. You don't push someone out; you don't stop loving or having feelings for someone. New ones just grow, like a new branch of a tree. It grows, develops, and spreads all on its own. Everything about the original tree and its branches stays the same, everything gets nourished. It just looks slightly different now.

We married five years after Steve passed. During that time, my dad had divorced his wife and was forging relationships with us. He had become the dad of our childhood again; I wanted my kids to have a relationship with their grandad. I knew how important those relationships were for me growing up. My dad, sister, and niece came to our wedding. We were a blended family of seven teens and young adults. I had mixed feelings about going through this again. Was I brave enough to take this journey, or more honestly, was I strong enough?

Four months after we married, he was diagnosed with cancer, colon cancer. I thought life was having a laugh at my expense. My mind stood still, and my heart went on autopilot. I closed my eyes for the tomorrows, I would have to manage this one day at a time. He was booked for surgery a few weeks later, my priest offered to come and sit with me that day. I could not think beyond that moment. I didn't want this to be my journey again. The surgery was longer and more intensive than originally planned; the surgeon was confident he had gotten everything out. Scans showed all clear margins. I wanted to breathe again, but I didn't dare. Trying to get back to a new normal was impossible, there was not an old normal to compare to. We all had pain and grief, it was all so different in context. Being on a journey through grief is very inimitable. My new husband was very different from Steve; he had high expectations in his parenting and was more authoritative. This was tough for my kids; they missed their dad. Our life, before Steve became Stage 4, was one of younger children, we were a goofy, messy, busy family, then we were trying to beat the clock. They didn't want a replacement, a "new" dad, they just wanted life to go back to how it was. My husband walked into a house of constant chaos and emotions. Standing up and trying to explain that different wasn't always bad, caused friction. Two of his four kids moved in with us, space was tight, and dinners were full and noisy. Those two kids adjusted amazingly; it was just super busy. Remembering life after my mum, stayed on my mind. I didn't want that for my kids, or his kids, and my husband was not the same as that either. I tried so hard to keep a balance, to stand up when needed. Blending a family is not easy, mix that with grief, emotions, and hormones, it can be a jumpy journey. We both had the same vision though, of healthy well-adjusted kids, who felt a solid base and were protected and loved. The kids were all getting older and parenting late teens is a futile exercise at best; we managed though, this road was never going to be easy, but we were all on it together.

THIRTEEN
THE LITTLE MATCH GIRL

Reinventing yourself, picking the shattered version of yourself, up, off the floor again; how many times can your soul do this? Memories of a lost childhood, a lost sisterhood, trying to rebuild those bonds, and heal the hurts. When do we get to feel safe to love again?

I remembered the last birthday I had at home with my younger sister. I was almost sixteen, she was twelve. Life was, in a nutshell, hell. My dad's girlfriend at that time, had us all terrified to move without her permission. Our dinner, when we were allowed to have it, was a small tin of beans or spaghetti hoops, she left on the bed. We had to beg for soap, shampoo, and a towel. Our clothes were being cut, ripped, torn, and thrown out. I knew I would be leaving as soon as I could, I was almost finished school. I searched for a book called The Little Match Girl by Hans Christian Anderson to give to my younger Sister as a birthday gift. It's a story about a poor young girl, trying to sell matches on the cold night streets at Christmas time. Fear of going home without selling anything kept her on the streets. Barefoot, and clothed in rags, she crouched in a corner, lighting the matches for warmth. As the matches glowed, she would see wonderful, warm visions of fireplaces, warmly decorated family homes, and large Christmas dinners. She sees a shooting star and remembers what her grandmother had told her: A shooting star is someone from heaven coming to carry you home. She lights all the matches at once, feeling the warmth and holding onto the vision as long as possible, before being carried to heaven by her grandmother. This story resonated with me, I didn't want to leave my younger sister in the cold, dark, loveless place she was in. I wanted her to see a bright and beautiful future; I wanted to take her in my arms and fly away to a place of warmth, love, and beauty. I bought her the book and a chocolate bar. The Little Match Girl and a Marathon, as they were called then. I froze the chocolate bar, so it wouldn't melt. I woke up early and crept into her bed, I read the story to her, and then we read it together. She always slept with dozens of small soft toys in her bed; we snuggled up with them, reading the book and looking at the illustrations over and over. We opened the chocolate bar and laughed with hysterics as we tried to eat this frozen Marathon. We chatted and laughed; it felt like being eight years old again, telling stories and singing songs to each other.

Eight years after Steve died, the kids had all moved on or out, university, jobs, partners; my heart was full of pride with how beautiful, well-adjusted, and balanced they all were, life was beginning to look like a new normal. My younger sister had just celebrated her first wedding anniversary. She had re-married, marrying the man she had always dreamt of, her soulmate; she was the happiest I had ever seen her.

I was visiting my mother-in-law when I got a call from

my dad. He very rarely, if ever, called me. I was a bit surprised but not super worried. "Are you sitting down?"

He repeated this a few times; I was curious; "Yes, I was already sitting down; why do you keep asking?"

He had repeated those words several times so as not to say the next ones. His hesitation froze me. "Your little sister is gone."

"What? That doesn't make any sense, where has she gone?"

He repeated, "She is gone. She passed."

I couldn't get my head around those words. My little sister, who just a year ago, had married her soulmate on a beautiful island beach. She was, for the first time in her entire life, truly happy, cared for, and loved. She was dead! I said the words out loud; I just ran, ran out of the building; those words kept echoing, echoing in my mind. My little sister, who finally has the life she deserves, is gone. I called my eldest sister; she was screaming on the phone; we screamed and cried together over the phone. We were five thousand miles apart, but screaming and crying as one. No one knew what had happened. She just died. She wasn't sick or injured; just died. I booked a flight back. Still not processing. I didn't have a return ticket, I didn't have a plan, I just needed to be back. I walked out of the airport. I saw my older sister. She put her hand to her face and came running to me. I dropped my bags, my body started to crumble as she reached me. We held onto each other, crying into each other's hearts.

PART 2

Still, I rise.
You may shoot me with your words,
You may cut me with your eyes,
You may kill me with your hatefulness,
But still, like air, I rise.
- Maya Angelo

You may want to journal or takes notes of your thoughts and feelings for this part. It is good to look back and see how far you come, and how much stronger, healthier and more resilient you have become.

FOURTEEN
THE JOURNEY

From the darkness to light.

The message of darkness to light and walking through Faith is about finding hope and guidance in times of struggle or uncertainty. It's about trusting in something greater than yourself, to lead you out of the darkness and into the light, relying on Faith to illuminate the past ahead, and overcome obstacles. It's a journey of perseverance, resilience, and transformation.

I have often felt that my life is in separate parts, the before and the after's. Before and after my mum died; before and after moving to Canada; before and after Steve died; before and after my sister died. Where did these parts of me begin and end? Did I change? Was I changed? Was loss a normal part of life? Why was my journey so jagged? It often felt as soon as I could see my path with the stones smooth and the road clear, there always appeared to be a roadblock. My mum's sister would say to me, "Our life is like a beautiful fairytale, our story is just not finished yet."

It seemed I never had a clear path. I was always stumbling from one disaster and heartache to the next. The fine intricacies of life had woven for me a map; a map I could only see when I looked back. Had my mum been so present, so strong and loving, so I could receive all she had to give in the thirteen short years she was with me? Did my nan become such an immense person in my life to teach me that life can hurt and you can still laugh? Did my mum die so young so I could follow my own journey and mother my own children? Without my mum dying so young would I have moved across the great pond? Would I have had the privilege of raising three strong amazing adults? Did my mum die, so I could feel the pain that my children felt when their dad died? The trauma of having abusive (step)mums, being taken advantage of by trusted adults, changed me. It led me on a path of self-destruction, anger, and despair; but it also made me fight stronger and harder for my own children.

There have been so many paths in my life, some with journeys I could have taken, but did not. Decisions that were so strong and present, that it took everything I had, not to follow them. How did I choose the paths that led me to my life, or away from another life? I sometimes wonder if I chose the paths, or was I gently guided. Where would I have been had I followed another journey or made a different decision? I have tried to raise my children with the lessons that had been taught to me, and had learned, but who from? Did I ever have a constant presence in my life that had guided me? My dad's mum, my nan was not related to me biologically, but she was my person. She still is the person that taught me so much about life, love, and laughter. She was always meant to be my nan and I was always meant to be her granddaughter. She loved her Faith, my nan wore a gold cross and chain every day, she held her Faith close. She loved and respected all religions. She saw the beauty in life, belief and Faith. I remember her telling me, when I was young, that if I wasn't christened, I would be a floating soul, with no resting place. When I finally saw Jesus in my heart, and became a child of God, I had Steve take a picture of that moment, the moment when my Priest baptized me, I then sent her that picture. I asked her once, how would I find her after death, she told me, "Wherever you are, I will be there too."

The path led me to Steve, and our children; it had led me to help my kids maintain a relationship with Steve's mum after he passed. It forged bridges with my dad, so my kids could know and love him. Without all the rocks and hurdles on my journey, would I be here? Are there experiences I wish I hadn't had, absolutely!! I wish my life had been smooth, uncomplicated, steady, boring and without heartache. That was not to be, and I am stronger for it. I am fierce in my love and honor, I make mistakes, huge mistakes, but I am easier on myself. I have found the gift of Faith and prayer, and it makes me stronger.

I can see my path clear when I look back, it has led me here. I can see the moments when I had to make a choice, make a decision. I can see my younger self standing there, indecisive, not knowing where to go next, I don't believe I was alone at those times. I had a gentleness, a guide, taking my hand and encouraging me forward. As I look back, I can see with pure clarity my journey, my path of life. Each road I took, each decision I made or chose not to make, had been taken with strength and Faith. I can look back and see a guiding hand, gently, encouragingly, urging me forward. I was never alone on my journey.

Task: Try to do this for 10mins a day, until it gets easier and the thoughts flow. Makes notes each time, so you can see your progress.

Find a quiet space, take some time, and look back on your life. See your journey as a whole; see those moments when a change occurred, new challenges arose, decisions were made, and clarity occurred. You may find this difficult at first, be easy on yourself if you cannot concentrate. If you feel blocks in your thoughts, take some breaths, and just be with yourself. Try to focus on a single memory, embrace it, feel it.

After some time, your thoughts will allow those memories that make you feel uncomfortable, think for a moment about them. What happened? How did you feel, and react? See where you changed course on your journey, did it take time, was it a slow gradual leave, how did you choose? Did you have a choice? Was there something encouraging you to move more one way than another? Were you alone in your thoughts and actions? Looking back, can you see your path clearer?

FIFTEEN
GRIEF

Matthew 5:4 *Blessed are those who mourn, for they will be comforted.*

Psalm 34:18 *The lord is close to the broken hearted and saves those who are crushed in spirit.*

Grieving someone while they are still living

How can Death be so different? Why is there both sadness and relief? For an older, sick person, someone in so much pain, it can be a relief. You don't want to see the suffering. Do you miss them any less? Absolutely not! Do you wish they were not suffering so death would be the relief? Of course! When a younger person, a child, innocent and pure, dies, it can be cruel and unfathomable. Why did this happen? Where was Jesus today? It does not make any sense why a young person should die. They not only lose their life; they lose their future. How do we reconcile this? Why do people say things happen for a reason, what was the reason here? We miss the child, we miss the person the child would become, we miss the milestones that were not met, the life experiences and changes having this person living could be. My baby cousin was trapped as a memory as someone he didn't get a chance to become.

To grieve someone who is still living, though: Is this even possible, what does it look like? When Steve and my mum's mum died, they both had been sick for a very long time. We were not saying goodbye to a healthy, vital person, they had lost the essence that was them. I remember one time, Steve and I were having a coffee in Niagara Falls, an elderly couple was bickering at the next table. It was a loving, have known you for forty years type of bicker. Steve looked at me, he said, "That will never be us, will it?"

It was heartbreaking but true. Steve had always shown optimism that he would beat the cancer. He wanted to live, he wanted to watch his children grow and meet his grandchildren. He would never get old. I would be living the rest of my life without him. This was not about me though, this was about keeping him with me, mentally and emotionally, for as long as I could. Once hope was lost for him, he became angry, self-pitying, the why me, what have I ever done wrong? Where is my God, and why has he failed me?

A cheerleader

Once this part of him was gone, once his essence was only a memory I could hold, I had to become his cheerleader, his caregiver, his protector; I was still his wife, and I missed the beautiful, strong, healthy person he was. I had to put aside my fears and give him all my strength to help him with as much grace and dignity as I could. I turned to my Faith, to Steve's Faith, to find the strength here. It was at this point I started to grieve my husband. Steve became very despondent, he was angry at what life had given him, scared for the future of myself and our children. Our Priest stopped by one morning; Steve asked him, "Why me? Why did I get Cancer, why do my kids have to grow up without a father?" It was heartbreaking to see this man, who was full of courage, strength, and hope, just break down and feel defeated. Our Priest sat close to Steve, held him, and said, "I know some people believe there are reasons for everything. And we all want to know why bad things happen to good people. But I have to be honest, I really don't know why so many people suffer in this world - why children go hungry, why people die in earthquakes. But I do take comfort in my Christian Faith. My Faith tells me that God does not leave us alone in our suffering but rather that God suffers with us. If Jesus was truly God, as Christians claim, then God was wrongfully arrested, tortured, and executed in a profoundly brutal way. He experienced the emotional pain of being cut off from family and the spiritual agony of feeling like his Heavenly Father had abandoned him. So, in Jesus, we know that God suffers with us. That does not magically take away our pain or make everything better. But I take comfort in believing that God is with us through all the challenges of his life and ultimately through his death."

These words profoundly affected him, knowing he wasn't alone in this journey and that Jesus was walking beside him in his pain, suffering, and heartache. I could see the change in him; the sadness and pain still enveloped him, but he was now stronger.

Endings happen all the time in life. Graduations, movies, and vacations are to name just a few. When you see the finish line, you start to make preparations, putting things in place for the ending. When movies wrap up, all the pieces of storylines start to come together and make sense, you can anticipate the next steps. Your journey home from holiday, finding that first grown-up job, moving to a new town. When you see the end of someone's life coming, it's a painful waiting game, not knowing the when, but knowing the how. You will have a list of people to call, and arrangements to be made, most of it is pre-planned and flows well. Your autopilot kicks in, and you deal with this stage, pretty much the same as you have dealt with all the other stages.

What no one tells you

What no one tells you is that everyone else moves on. They go home, back to work, and back to school; they have dealt with this inevitable event; they have visited, done their due service, and went home. You will find yourself sitting alone in the dark, thinking, "What now, What's next?" You have to wake up each morning and continue to do life. The hardest part of losing my husband was waking up every day without him, without purpose, without companionship. Trying to keep myself intact and strong for my children, I was broken, but I couldn't be broken. When I felt myself digging that deep pit, I would pray for strength, faith, and healing. I wanted to run away when I found myself falling, I had to constantly remind myself to stay, to stand still, tall, and strong; even when I couldn't, I had to pretend. I still pray for strength and healing, but I still find myself falling, broken, and shattered. I will close my eyes and feel the rush of sadness and despair wash over me. Only now, it's less frequent and less deep, I can pull myself up faster. I now know I will get through this moment, and I will be stronger for it.

Task: In your journal, write your late loved one a letter. Pour all your feelings and tears into it. Don't hold back. It may look like a ramble of disjointed words. Some may be angry, harsh, broken, words of forgiveness, words of asking for forgiveness, words of love, honor, courage, and sadness. These are your thoughts, your letter, there is no wrong or right here. Date it, and put it away. You can revisit when you're feeling stronger when some time has passed. Has any of those words found resolve? Do this exercise once in a while, (maybe six months or yearly) and look back on your path of healing. How are you feeling after you have written a few times?

SIXTEEN
THE INNOCENCE OF CHILDHOOD

Part 1 - Innocent Memories

Isaiah 24:13-14 and 17. *All our children shall be taught by the Lord and great will be their peace, their health, safety, protection, and prosperity. In righteousness, they will be established. Tyranny will be far from them; they will have nothing to fear, terror will be far removed; it will not come near them.*

I loved being a kid, I had a good childhood, we were pretty poor and tangled; but life was good and I was happy. Over the past forty years, I have often thought of the time I saw my childhood dog, Saber, being taken to heaven in a basket with angels, I was around three at the time, I don't think I even told anyone what I saw until my teen years, then it was, "You have a wild imagination!" But did I? I recently sat down with my priest and talked about this. I laughed it off as a child trying to make sense of something she didn't understand. He said to me something like, just because it doesn't make sense doesn't mean it wasn't real.

That had me thinking, does our child-like mind try to make sense of grown-up things, or is our child-like mind so innocent and pure that we can see things truly as they are? I knew nothing of religion or Faith at this age, had never been to church; Angels sat on top of Christmas trees. So why did I see my beloved dog be taken up, into the sky, in a basket, with angels?

Task: Do you remember anything as a small child that is unexplainable that could not possibly have happened? Have you noticed coincidences in life with no explanation? Think about these moments. Sit down with your own thoughts, and think, write about anything you never really quite understood. Does it make sense now? Was this just your childhood imagination, or maybe Jesus helping you to understand and make sense of a difficult moment?

Part 2 - When trust turns to fear: Grooming and stepparent tyranny

2 Corinthians 12:9-10 *But, He said to me, 'My grace is sufficient for you, for my power is made perfect in weakness' so that Christ's power may rest on me. That is why, for Christ's sake, I delight in weakness, in insults, in hardships, in persecutions, in difficulties. For when I am weak, then I am strong.*

Grown-ups: As children we tend to trust the grown-ups in our lives. The teachers, our friend's parents, family members, neighbors, and our parent's friends. They are older, and in authority, we have a natural tendency to do as they say, follow their direction, respect their decisions, and place our trust in them.

Grooming

This is typically when a trusted adult attempts to build a relationship with a child, to gain their trust, and to develop an emotional attachment with the intent of exploiting them emotionally, physically, or sexually. ..."To avoid discovery, they tend to control their victims through this grooming process." - Kenneth Lanning MS (The evolution of grooming). An adult, who was supposedly a close family friend, who was taking a role in our lives after my mum died, was stepping over boundaries, making me feel unsafe, uncomfortable and vulnerable. I often thought fear and embarrassment protected here. I was scared and confused. What made me run, what made me hide? I could hear a tiny voice in my head saying "Stop" "No" "Run" I was thirteen/fourteen years old. These were people who had loved my mum, so why was I scared? I had to trust my instincts, and they were telling me to leave. I felt a gentle guiding hand, nudging me to safety. I look back and see Jesus' hand gently guiding me. Aly McDonnell wrote in her book (Walking out of Shame: A woman's journey to finding self-love after childhood sexual abuse) - *Today, when I look back on my life, I can see that I was never truly "unsafe." Not really. After all, here I am, unbroken, complete, whole. The essence of what I am has never been damaged.* ... The wholeness I saw within me, had no need to argue with the truth of what happened.

Task: Have you ever felt that uncomfortable feeling, itchiness inside your soul, telling you to go, change direction, walk a different path? Take a moment to think and confront those memories and feelings. What do you think this was? Intuition? Jesus? A bigger-than-life presence? Did you listen and change your direction? Looking back, can you see this clearer than when you were in it? What were your reactions? Write down how you felt, what you did, and what you wish you had done. Can you confront this person, will it resolve anything? Will it make any difference? Write in your journal a letter to this person that made you feel unsafe. Be descriptive and don't hold back on your word choice. (This letter is for you, not to send, unless you feel compelled to.) Put all your feelings down. How does this make you feel? Close your journal. Revisit this page in the next few months, only if you want to. Write down words to take back control, to heal your inner child, to be stronger. Don't let this perpetrator rent any more space in your head. You will get stronger, you will see this person as weak, vulnerable, manipulative, and inadequate. You will rise and be stronger and stop this cycle of abuse.

Stepparents

These are adults put in a position of expected authority in our lives; we are not supposed to question them. As children, we follow our parent's rules, even when we feel they are wrong. To challenge your parental figure can put you at risk and make you feel vulnerable, angry, and very much alone. We are supposed to trust and be loved by our family. Does love look like this in life, it can be confusing. Being a child grieving the loss of my mum, I was in desperate need of that parental love that was missing. Often, the introduction of a new (step) parent will bring feelings of loss, confusion, and emotional turmoil to the surface. New family dynamics must be navigated with support, patience, and empathy. In my circumstance the (step) parents were emotionally, verbally, and physically abusive, the dynamics became unsafe and toxic very quickly. This abuse often looked like verbal abuse: swearing, belittling, snide comments, name-calling. They can confuse the situations and undermine us, making us feel confused, insecure, and doubtful of our own perceptions.

The (step) parent may spread rumors and lies to the child's support network, creating isolation and further dependence on the abuser. The child can be left feeling unloved, unwanted, alone, misunderstood, with low self-esteem, depression, anxiety, and have issues learning to trust and build intimate relationships. What makes a (step) parent behave like this? I have often thought of it as spite and jealousy, especially if there are biological children of the (step) parent. That they want all the love and riches to go to their own children, and to take away from that leaves their children wanting. It's like, putting women and children on a lifeboat first, and only the men if there is room.

The non-bio children will often get left behind, with scraps of love and attention. The Cinderella effect theory has long been discussed in psychology and anthropology, where stepmothers are more likely to abuse and/or neglect their stepchildren and not their biological children. How do we come to terms with this form of abuse and alienation? How do we, as those children, find hope, light, and strength? I was lucky and old enough to leave. Not everyone had that opportunity for many years. How do we resolve these feelings?

Task: Write about your thoughts, be brutal and honest with your feelings and your experience. Keep going back to your journaling, tracking your thoughts, feelings, and emotions of this time. Understand that this was not about you, this said nothing of who you were or are. This was all about them, the abuser. I see them as feeling vulnerable and inadequate, wanting to subjugate a child to empower themselves, speaks volumes of their own limitations. The same as in grooming, write your abuser a letter, laying all the hurt, anger, despair, and ugly feelings down. You don't have to send this, just get it out and on paper. Put it aside, and re-visit months later, when you are feeling stronger. Do you see the lightness here, are you emerging from the darkness of the tunnel to become stronger, more vital, more powerful?

SEVENTEEN
FORGIVENESS

Self-forgiveness:

Psalm 103:12 *As far as the east is from the west, so far has He removed our transgressions against us.*

This is a hard one: Forgive yourself. Say that again. Forgive yourself. We all live ordinary lives, have good days, bad days, say things we regret in anger or frustration. In a perfect world, we would have all the right words, feels and emotions. The world is not perfect, we cannot always be perfect. Have you ever said or done something you regretted, like something really stupid when you were hurt, angry or frustrated. We don't intend to hurt the people we love. We can be so wrapped up in our own lives, that we can't see what is happening around us. This is not intentional, in someways, we try to protect ourselves by shutting people out, not taking on their pain, as we cannot cope with our own. Sometimes after harsh words, arguments, fights, bad feelings, crappy days, a person may die unexpectedly. Those last words you say to someone does not sum up the entire relationship you had with them. Those are words. They are lost. Forgive yourself. You do not stop caring for someone because they were an asshole that day. They were just being an ass. As that saying goes - Every day I love you more, except yesterday, yesterday you were an idiot. - anonymous If you had one more day, or moment, with your person, would it have changed much, not knowing what was to come? Would that fight you had, those bad words exchanged, the flipping the bird behind their back, change anything? In reality, those moments would have been forgotten, and life would have moved on. But that didn't happen. They died, those words, thoughts, and feelings cannot be taken back. Cannot be resolved. It's okay. They knew how you felt, you knew how they felt. Forgive yourself.

Task: I want you to close your eyes. Think of that moment you regret. Not just the words, but the whole emotion. Think how you were feeling. The words said, from you, and also maybe to you. How does this make you feel? What emotions are running through your mind? Your heart? Quietly, to that person in your thoughts, say sorry. Ask for self-forgiveness, and pray for self-forgiveness. Understand that this was a moment, one moment. Let it go. With practice, you will find freedom of the demon in your thoughts, you will begin healing.

To forgive unintended hurt

Luke 23:34 *Father forgive them, for they do not know what they are doing.*

People in our lives can hurt us without intent. Situations happen and can be out of our control. My family not stepping in and protecting us was not intentional. All of us were navigating our journey of grief, trying our best to follow our own journey and move forward. I didn't understand until my own sister died how completely broken my aunt was when her sister, my Mum, died. It all makes so much sense to me now. Forgiving someone else's behavior can be hard until you understand it. Sometimes, you may just need to let go. I personally do not need to forgive my dad for not seeing or understanding the physical, verbal, and emotional abuse his two partners put us through. He was also grieving, a sudden widow with three children to raise; he wasn't coping well. For me, I can't excuse him for turning a blind eye, but I do understand it. There was nothing to forgive, he didn't hurt us, he just wasn't emotionally strong enough at that point. Once he began to see with clear eyes, things changed; the dad of my childhood returned. The goofy, grumpy, spoilt, nothing is ever serious Dad. My kids told me a while back, that their Grandad is the funniest person in our family. It took about twenty-five years to happen, but it did.

To forgive intentional hurt

A person can intentionally hurt us; they can physically, emotionally, psychologically, verbally, sexually, and even financially abuse us. This can be done with purpose and intent. Maybe to fulfill their own sick needs out of spite or jealousy. They may be taking advantage of a more vulnerable person, maybe someone with developmental, emotional, or physical challenges, someone who is grieving and cannot see the world straight. or just because. This speaks volumes of the abuser; I see this abuser as weak.

Forgiveness here is harder; I cannot forgive or forget the behavior, but I can find peace, let go, and move on. The heart can be ready to stop rehashing the person's behavior towards us, to stop us from being trapped in those past moments of trauma. Thinking about the would haves, should haves, the self-blame, the ugly self-feelings, vulnerability, self-loathing. Attitudinal forgiveness is forgiving someone when they do not acknowledge or admit to any wrongdoing. This, for me, looks like forgiving this person before God or in your own heart. I pray that I am eased from this burden and that the feelings of hatred, sadness, and despair are replaced with peace and freedom. Freedom from being trapped in those memories and moments.

Task: Find a quiet space where you can be with your thoughts. Write your thoughts and emotions down if you find this helps. You can begin with just a few minutes and increase as you get stronger. Eventually, you will feel relief and clarity. You will find freedom in your thoughts and begin to get stronger.

Sit quietly and think about the person/persons who hurt you; think about the physical, emotional, and psychological harm that they did and how it has affected your life so far. Think of prayer to let go of those thoughts, feelings, and emotions. Free yourself, take back control this person has had in your life. You are freeing yourself by letting go of the thoughts and the pain that haunt you. Healing doesn't mean the pain never existed. It means it can no longer control your life.

EIGHTEEN
HEALING

Isaiah 40:29-31 *He gives strength to the weary and increases power to the weak, even youths grow tired and weary, and young men stumble and fall: but those who hope in the Lord will renew their strength, they will soar on wings like eagles; they will run and not grow weary, they will walk and not be faint.*

In Grief

They say time heals. I don't believe this is completely true. The more time that passes, the more memories are missed. Birthdays, births, weddings, and holidays, the absence of someone becomes increasingly apparent. We will journey through life, having experiences and making memories that we will never be able to share, that they will never be a part of. This does not mean you will forever be in that moment. That dark place of grief. The pain hurts like a knife wound, but it will heal. The scar will always be there, hidden, like a reminder, a badge of honor for loving someone. I can often look at photos, really look at them deeply, study the contour of their face, their eyes; I can hear the laughter, and their voice resonates inside me; it's as if, for a moment, they have been brought back to me.

We don't "get over" losing someone special to us. They never leave us. We will always miss them, that specialness that made them. To honor someone is to miss them and keep a special moment in our hearts. Understanding and embracing that is key to healing. We will always want them here. Most days, we can be happy and sad at the same time. That is okay. Your journey through loss is yours alone. We all walk this path at some point in our lives. We often do not walk this path alone. Just because someone you love dies; the love you have for that person doesn't leave. I miss many people; some have passed, and some are still very much alive. I can reach out to the people I miss who are alive, have a quick chat with, plan a visit, and make a connection that brings us together. Oftentimes, I want to wait until tomorrow; life gets busy, and there is always another day. A missed text, forgotten voicemail, quick birthday. "Hi, we should get together soon."

That soon can lead to weeks, months, sometimes longer. When someone dies, though, it often feels like we need to connect with them more. It becomes urgent and emotional that we never got to say or do that last thing. We may be reaching into our memories to find a moment with them. It is hard to accept that the moments are now gone. What does healing look like? It can be so different for each person who has lost someone and for each person who we have lost. Acceptance is one, to know cognitively that someone is gone, to acknowledge the presence and experience of a person gone. Your mind moves forward, your heart creates a Band-Aid. The pain and anguish decrease. You can think of this person with more clarity and less pain. You will never stop missing them or wanting them, you just come to a level of acceptance. I have had moments of pure acceptance and then not, I seem to regress to the hurt, pain, denial, missing, flood of tears. This happens less frequently, and I am able to pull myself together faster. But forty years after my mum died, I can still be that girl, running to the back garden to escape reality. My eldest child's partner recently created a picture of my mum on wood. It was from a time before I knew my mum when she was a teenager. Seeing it was like a bolt of memories flooding my mind and heart, it took my breath away. I gave myself a private moment to cherish those feelings. It felt like a new moment when I could love my mum.

Task/Reflection: People seem to want you to talk about your grief, has this helped you at all? Have you talked to anyone and actually felt better? I have a personal rule with talking about my grief. I can only talk about it when I am ready to and for as long as I need. I cannot talk on demand, or to people that I don't want to that day. It has taken years of practice to be open about this, and be able to speak more freely. Some people will think that because you don't talk about it, then you are essentially over it. I believe the opposite is more true. To talk about your trauma/grief, while it's still raw, is too hard, it's only as the heart heals that you can be more vulnerable and open.

Healing through trauma

For me, the first step of healing through my trauma was to acknowledge it. I have been so angry for so long that it was hard for me to go back and see where it all came from. I had to open doors to wounds that had long been closed. Dissecting and confronting my past has been liberating. For the first time in over four decades, I can see. I am not broken because my mum died; I am broken because the adults around me, who I presumed were there to help and protect me after she died, didn't. They took a vulnerable pre-teen and exploited their control over her. They stepped into a parenting role and abused her. They made her feel less than, unworthy, unloved, rejected, and disregarded. Becoming a mum, with only the memory of a strong mother and examples of abusive (step)parents, was difficult. I had to trust my inner instincts to nurture, protect, and love my children. I wanted to give them all the love, attachment, and nurturing that I could. I never wanted them to feel alone, sad, broken. Losing Steve shook that up, and I fell into a pit of despair again. I was failing as a mother, and it cut my heart so deeply. My Faith and prayers were so jumbled, I didn't know what to even pray for anymore. Slowly, I began to think about my past, rebuilding my relationships with my family, owning my part in the destruction, and allowing myself to remember and feel my past pain. I began to think about my pain, think about what happened, why it happened, who was in control, did I do anything to make it happen. I would talk about it, at first, just to myself, then in my prayers, then slowly to my family. I began to write things down. Sometimes I would get so lost in my thoughts that my mind would start spinning, other memories would come, and it became so overwhelming that I had to walk away for a bit. Confronting my fears, my demons, laying them bare, open, for all to see, the ugliness, the rawness, owning my anger and hurt; only then did my healing truly begin.

Task: It is hard to begin to heal unless you acknowledge and learn from your trauma. Ask yourself, are you still angry, are you looking to heal, or are you allowing yourself to succumb to your anger and the pain? We continually look for the answers, but there are none, which is why we have to channel the energy from anger and pain to coping and healing. Open up your journal and start taking notes of your thoughts and feelings. Date your entries so you can look back and see how much progress you have made on your journey. Think about those moments, those triggers that take you back to your grief, back to your trauma. Have you noticed less intensity, a shorter period of time that you are lost in this place? Do you feel stronger and more capable? Think about these questions, look back, and reflect on your journey. Write a short note to yourself about where you are in your healing journey today. Put this away, and put a reminder in your calendar for six months, a year from now. Then, when the time comes, re-read, and reflect. Are you in that same place? What has taken place to aid or stop your healing? Add it to your note, and put it away for another six months - a year.

NINETEEN
MOVING FORWARD

Philippians 4:6-7 *Do not be anxious about anything, but in every situation, by prayer and petition, with thanksgiving, present your requests to God. And the peace of God, which transcends all understanding, will guard your hearts and your minds in Christ Jesus.*

When someone you love passes on, you don't have the concrete ability to connect with them. You miss them more on some days than others. Sometimes, the feelings are so overwhelming that it can be a moment or an entire day. They stay in your mind and heart. You can think about them, talk to them silently, show them things in your heart. They stay with you, always, and every time you need them, you feel them. You will miss them, though. Everyday. After my sister died, her ashes were scattered on the island where she was married. On what would have been her fiftieth birthday, we all went there. My younger sister had no Faith and did not believe in God or any religion for that matter. I walked into the ocean and lay on my back, my entire body submersed, except the small of my face. I could feel the ocean moving me and see the sky, the clouds, and the outline of the mountains in the distance. I marveled at the infinite beauty of this place. I closed my eyes and lost myself in prayer for my sister. Praying for her peace and freedom of all those years she went through, praying that she would now be with our mum, our grandparents, and yes, Steve. I prayed in acknowledgment of those last years she lived, being the best and happiest she had. An amazing husband, a beautiful grown child, and two wonderful bonus adult kids. I mourned with her, the future she lost, the future we all lost with her. I did this several times while we were there, keeping her close to my thoughts and heart. I felt a sense of peace; I felt that she was at peace, that we could continue our journey through life with her memory tucked safely in our hearts. You don't stop loving someone just because they are no longer there. Love is an emotion, a feeling, not an object. The person has gone, but all that love stays. It becomes a huge emotional ball that hurts for a long time, then it tucks itself away somewhere safe, somewhere you can still feel it, when you need to. It will never disappear completely. We love so many people in our lives. Parents, aunts, uncles, siblings, cousins, friends, children. Our love for each of these people does not get diluted. It doesn't thin out. When you have one child, your heart explodes like you have never experienced. You truly think you cannot love anyone as much. Then you have a second, a third, maybe a fourth even. Your heart just expands and grows to allow more love in. Your capacity for love is endless. You can fall in love with someone else and still love your lost person as much. Moving forward is not always the same as moving on. You will have new experiences, enjoy new memories, meet new people, fall in love again. Your new love does not diminish the love you shared before. It stands apart from it, and grows. When my dad's mum became ill, I wrote her a letter. I wanted her to know that even though we were not biologically related, her presence in my life would continue on in my children. The love she gave, the lessons I learned, and the support and strength I felt from her all contributed to how I mothered my children. We would not inherit genetic traits, but we would inherit values and beliefs which has and will continue to shape our identity and worldviews.

Billy Bob Thornton said about the loss of his brother: "I've never been the same since my brother died. There's a melancholy in me that never goes away, I am fifty percent happy and fifty percent sad at any given moment(...) I don't want to forget what it felt like when he died because he deserves that remembrance; that's how important he was to me. (...) I'll be sad and melancholy about that forever, and I accept it, and I live with it, but I think that's okay. It's okay to have all those feelings."

Task: I want you to think of several, maybe between two to four good memories. Write them down, then take a deep dive into your thoughts with them, one at a time. The location, atmosphere, scents, conversations, and even the weather. Take a moment and embrace the memory. Think about your thoughts, feelings, and emotions that day. Reminisce and sunbathe in them. Remembering the love you shared with someone is so precious. Remembering the joy they brought to life and the very essence of themselves. Each person is a gift in our life; hold that gift close to your heart. Samara, Lisa M, in Our Daily Bread (Thursday March 7, 2024) God's protection comes from his mighty strength, as well as His tenderness and love, which causes Him too long to provide refuge to the hurting. For all who are struggling, our heavenly Father offers a place of refuge in His strength and tenderness.

Printed in Dunstable, United Kingdom

63471637R00078